Managing Projects with make

Managing Projects with make

Andrew Oram and Steve Talbott

O'REILLY®

Beijing · Cambridge · Farnham · Köln · Paris · Sebastopol · Taipei · Tokyo

Managing Projects with make
by Andrew Oram and Steve Talbott

Editor: Steve Talbott

Printing History:

1986:	First Edition by Steve Talbott.
August 1987:	Minor corrections. Index added. Revised page design by Linda Lamb and Dale Dougherty.
July 1988:	Minor corrections.
October 1989:	Minor corrections.
March 1990:	Minor corrections.
January 1991:	Minor corrections.
October 1991:	Second Edition. Revised and expanded by Andrew Oram.
December 1991:	Minor corrections.
February 1993:	Minor corrections.

ISBN: 0-937175-90-0   [1/01]
[M]

Table of Contents

Page

Preface ix

The Value of make x
Lessons from make xi
Variants xi
Scope of This Book xii
Getting Automated Tests xiii
FTP xiii
FTPMAIL xiv
BITFTP xv
UUCP xvi
Conventions Used in This Handbook xvi
Acknowledgments xvii
We'd Like to Hear From You xvii

Chapter 1 How to Write a Simple Makefile 1

The Description File 2
Dependency Checking 3
Minimizing Rebuilds 4
Invoking make 5
Basic Rules of Syntax 7

Chapter 2 Macros 9

Syntax Rules 10
Internally Defined Macros 12
Macro Definitions on the Command Line 13
Shell Variables 13
Priority of Macro Assignments 14
Relying on Environment Variables for Defaults 16

Macro String Substitution 18
Internal Macros for Prerequisites and Targets 19

Chapter 3 Suffix Rules 23

What is a Suffix Rule? 24
   Command Options 26
   Internal Macros 27
Commands Supported by Default Suffix Rules 28
   Fortran and Pascal 28
   SCCS and RCS 29
   Libraries (Archives) 33
   Using Parentheses for Library Modules 35
   A Library Example 36
   Maintaining Libraries 37
   The Double Colon 37
   lex and yacc 38
   The Null Suffix 39
How to Display Defaults 39
   Generating the Display 40
   What the Display Means 40
Writing Your Own Suffix Rules 48
   A Sample Collection of Suffix Rules 49
   Nullifying Rules 54
   Conflicts With Default Suffixes 56

Chapter 4 Commands 57

Filename Pattern Matching 58
Effects of Newlines on Commands 59
Errors and Exit Status 61
Which Shell? 64
Pathnames and Security 65

Chapter 5 Project Management 67

Dummy Targets 68
Recursive make on Directories 70
General Tips on Recursive make 72
Other Techniques for Multiple Directories 74
   Directories in Internal Macros 74
   Viewpath (VPATH Macro) 75
Compiler Options and #ifdef directives 78
   Forcing Remakes 80
   Maintaining Multiple Variants Through Explicit Targets 83
   Maintaining Multiple Variants in Different Directories 83
   Maintaining Variants Through Suffix Rules 85
Header Files 85
Global Definitions (include Statement) 88
Distributed Files and NFS Issues 89

Chapter 6 Command-line Usage and Special Targets 93

Description Filenames 94
Status Information and Debugging 94
Errors and File Deletion 96
The MAKEFLAGS Macro 96
Miscellaneous Features Affecting Defaults 97

Chapter 7 Troubleshooting 99

Debugging a Build (-d Option) 99
Syntax Errors 101
Don't Know How to Make 101
Target Up to Date 102
Command Not Found, or Cannot Load 103
Syntax Errors in Multi-line Commands 105
Inconsistent Lines, or Too Many Lines 106
Unrecognized Macros 107
Default Rules Ignored 108

Appendix A Quick Reference 109

Command Line 109
Description File Lines 110
Macros 112
   Internal Macros 112
   Macro Modifiers 113
   Macro String Substitution 113
   Macros with Special Handling 113
Special Target Names 113

Appendix B Popular Extensions 115

mk and nmake 116
GNU make 118
imake 119
makedepend 122
shape 123
Parallel and Distributed Implementations 125

Appendix C Features That Differ Between Variants of make 127

Background 128
List of Differences 128
Tests You Can Run 130
   Macro String Substitution 130
   File and Directory Macros 130
   Target Name as $$@ on Dependency Lines 130
   Parenthesis Syntax for Libraries 131
   Single-suffix Rules and .sh Rules 132
   Default Shell 133
   MAKE and MAKEFLAGS Macros 134
   include Statement 134
   VPATH 134

Index 137

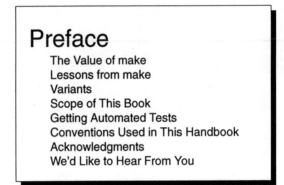

Preface

The Value of make
Lessons from make
Variants
Scope of This Book
Getting Automated Tests
Conventions Used in This Handbook
Acknowledgments
We'd Like to Hear From You

make is a command generator. Using a description file and some general templates, it creates a sequence of commands for execution by the UNIX shell. These commands commonly relate to the maintenance of the files comprising a software development project. "Maintenance" refers to a whole array of tasks, ranging from status reporting and the purging of temporary files, to building the final, executable version of a complex group of programs.

make is most naturally used to sort out dependency relations among files. Even relatively small software projects typically involve a number of files that depend upon each other in various ways. For example, a program must be linked from object files and libraries, which in turn must be created from assembly language or high-level language source files. If you modify one or more source files, you must relink the program after recompiling some—but not necessarily all—of the sources. This selective building is normally repeated many times during the course of a project.

It is this process that *make* greatly simplifies. You record once and for all the relationships among a set of files and then let *make* automatically perform all updating tasks. You need only issue a command having this general form:

```
$ make myprog
```

make then carries out only those tasks necessitated by project work since the previous *make* command. It achieves this in part by examining the file system to determine when the relevant files were last modified. If file A depends on file B, and if B was modified after A, then A must be "remade"—compiled, linked, edited, substituted in a library, or whatever.

The Value of make

The UNIX operating system earned its reputation above all by providing an unexcelled environment for software development. The *make* and *sccs* utilities are widely regarded as the greatest contributors to the efficiency of this environment. Although the immense growth of the computer industry and the increasing scale of software projects reveal limitations in these tools, most of their potential successors are just extensions along the lines of principles established by *make* and *sccs*.

The basics of *make* can be learned fairly quickly. You may well regain the time spent reading this book whenever you type the command

```
$ make myprog
```

But the value of *make* goes beyond saving time. Modern software development is centered on teamwork. By keeping track of dependency relationships among the parts of large, complex projects, *make* helps coordinate the efforts of many contributors. Many development teams could not pursue their day-to-day activities without it.

Few tools are applied in as wide a variety of situations as *make*. Although its principal domain is C programming, people who become familiar with *make* in that context soon start to find completely different spheres of activity in which to apply it. At many sites *make* has spread to general use for software installation, document formatting, and cleaning out temporary files.

Lessons from make

While you can get a lot out of just using *make* to automate frequently-used commands, it rewards each additional quantum of effort that you invest in studying its operation. As you learn to exploit its subtler features, you can also learn about programming conventions of UNIX systems. In its assumptions about parsing command lines and interpreting filenames, *make* reveals the standards enforced by shells and utilities.

make is also interesting as a programming concept. Although an individual entry executes sequentially, the overall method is non-procedural. The commands to be executed are determined by an iterative process of tracing the dependencies of the files you want to build. Thus, *make* is the only utility in common use that demonstrates the concepts of logic programming languages such as Prolog.

Variants

As one would expect with a utility that is intimately tied to its environment, *make* has evolved continuously since its inception. Thus, many useful features have been added by various implementors after *make* had time to spread and to develop into different variants. These features are too valuable to ignore, but their use definitely reduces the portability of your description files. Points of divergence can unfortunately be subtle, either because implementors felt free to change a new feature according to their personal tastes, or simply because documentation was sketchy and ambiguous (until this book, of course).

The System V Release 4 version of *make*, distributed by AT&T, forms the basis of this book. We have chosen this version because its features have been stable for some time and are available on most modern UNIX systems. We have tried to be careful to include caveats for features that might not have made it on to some systems—particularly the Berkeley Standard Distribution (BSD)—or that might be implemented differently. Appendix C provides a little history and a list of features subject to variation.

It's worth trying the features in this book even if the documentation for your system fails to list them. You might find that they work. Many programmers have added features to *make* without updating the documentation.

Almost every implementation of *make* contains a few enhancements that have not been brought back into the standard System V distribution. We could not possibly describe all these enhancements, particularly as the features are scattered among different variants and often get changed slightly during a port. But after reading this book, you should be able to recognize useful features in the documentation for your version of *make*, and see how to apply them to your needs.

Scope of This Book

Our goal is to help you become a productive user of standard *make* features. We hope that the book takes you as far as you want to explore. You can learn the main features of *make* quickly, along with just enough background to avoid frustrating mistakes. You can then come back to the book when you need to understand the more obscure features and underlying principles of operation.

Chapter 1, *How to Write a Simple Makefile*, explains the basic elements of a *make* description file, and leads you step by step through the creation of a simple description file. It explains the terms *target* and *prerequisite*, and discusses the commands *make* generates. After reading this chapter, you will be able to use *make* for many of its most common purposes.

Chapter 2, *Macros*, discusses macros and shell variables, and explains how the shell environment affects description files. It includes information about most of *make*'s internal macros.

Chapter 3, *Suffix Rules*, covers the rather large subject of suffix lists and suffix rules. Understanding this material will enable you to see how *make* accomplishes so much of its work automatically, as if by magic. You will also learn how to write your own suffix rules.

Chapter 4, *Commands*, examines in more detail the commands that you put in your description file. Although most commands work the way they would when you enter them at a terminal, some subtle and critical differences can prove frustrating until you understand how *make* interprets commands and uses shells.

Chapter 5, *Project Management*, builds on the basic information in earlier chapters to show how to use *make* in large, modern development projects. This chapter points out the major areas of difficulty—multiple directories, compiler options, and hidden dependencies—and then introduces the most popular solutions and workarounds. Topics include recursive invocations of *make*, the use of dummy targets, the VPATH macro, and automatic generation of header file dependencies.

Chapter 6, *Command-line Usage and Special Targets*, covers some miscellaneous command-line options and targets that have special, built-in meanings.

Chapter 7, *Troubleshooting*, presents some guidelines for figuring out what is wrong when *make* reports an error or simply does not do what you expect.

Appendix A, *Quick Reference*, summarizes the description file syntax, command-line options, and internal macros in standard *make*.

Appendix B, *Popular Extensions*, describes some of the *make* extensions and preprocessors that are available free of charge. Here we also mention current industry trends such as those leading to parallel and distributed *make* implementations.

Appendix C, *Features That Differ Between Variants of make*, briefly describes the evolution of *make*, summarizes the most common differences between variants, and provides some simple tests you can run to find out how your variant behaves.

Getting Automated Tests

The tests for *make* variants discussed in Appendix C have been incorporated into shell scripts. These scripts simply create a few small files, run *make* commands as shown in the appendix, and report the results to the standard output. The tests are available in a number of ways: by *ftp*, *ftpmail*, *bitftp*, and *uucp*. The cheapest, fastest, and easiest ways are listed first. If you read from the top down, the first one that works for you is probably the best. Use *ftp* if you are directly on the Internet. Use *ftpmail* if you are not on the Internet but can send and receive electronic mail to internet sites (this includes CompuServe users). Use BITFTP if you send electronic mail via BITNET. Use UUCP if none of the above works.

Although these tests have been run on several systems, we cannot guarantee them. There are many variants of *make*, and it is extremely dependent on its environment. If you notice behavior on your system that the tests do not understand or handle properly, please let us know and we will try to upgrade the tests to cover the behavior.

FTP

To use FTP, you need a machine with direct access to the Internet. A sample session is shown, with what you should type in boldface.

```
% ftp ftp.oreilly.com
Connected to ftp.oreilly.com.
220 FTP server (Version 6.21 Tue Mar 10 22:09:55 EST 1992) ready.
Name (ftp.oreilly.com:username): anonymous
331 Guest login ok, send domain style e-mail address as password.
```

```
Password: username@hostname (use your user name and host here)
230 Guest login ok, access restrictions apply.
ftp> cd /published/oreilly/nutshell/make
250 CWD command successful.
ftp> binary (Very important! You must specify binary transfer for compressed files.)
200 Type set to I.
ftp> get make.tar.Z
200 PORT command successful.
150 Opening BINARY mode data connection for make.tar.Z.
226 Transfer complete.
ftp> quit
221 Goodbye.
%
```

If the file is a compressed tar archive, extract the files from the archive by typing:

```
% zcat make.tar.Z | tar xf -
```

System V systems require the following tar command instead:

```
% zcat make.tar.Z | tar xof -
```

If *zcat* is not available on your system, use separate *uncompress* and *tar* commands.

FTPMAIL

FTPMAIL is a mail server available to anyone who can send and COPYRIGHTre-ceive electronic mail to and from Internet sites. This includes any company or service provider that allows email connections to the Internet. Here's how to do it.

You send mail to *ftpmail@online.ora.com*. In the message body, give the *ftp* commands you want to run. The server will run anonymous *ftp* for you and mail the files back to you. To get a complete *help* file, send a message with no subject and the single word "help" in the body. The following is an example mail session that should get you the examples. This command sends you a listing of the files in the selected directory, and the requested examples file. The listing is useful if there's a later version of the examples you're interested in.

```
% mail ftpmail@online.ora.com
Subject:
reply-to username@hostname          (Where you want files mailed)
open
cd /published/oreilly/nutshell/make
dir
mode binary
uuencode                            (or btoa if you have it)
```

```
get make.tar.Z
quit
.
```

A signature at the end of the message is acceptable as long as it appears after "quit."

All retrieved files will be split into 60KB chunks and mailed to you. You then remove the mail headers and concatenate them into one file, and then *uudecode* or *atob* it. Once you've got the desired file, follow the directions under FTP to extract the files from the archive.

BITFTP

BITFTP is a mail server for BITNET users. You send it electronic mail messages requesting files, and it sends you back the files by electronic mail. BITFTP currently serves only users who send it mail from nodes that are directly on BITNET, EARN, or NetNorth. BITFTP is a public service of Princeton University. Here's how it works.

To use BITFTP, send mail containing your *ftp* commands to *BITFTP@PUCC*. For a complete *help* file, send HELP as the message body.

The following is the message body you should send to BITFTP:

```
FTP  ftp.oreilly.com . NETDATA
USER  anonymous
PASS your Internet email address (not your bitnet address)
CD  /published/oreilly/nutshell/make
DIR
BINARY
GET  make.tar.Z
QUIT
```

Once you've got the desired file, follow the directions under FTP to extract the files from the archive. Since you are probably not on a UNIX system, you may need to get versions of *uudecode*, *uncompress*, *atob*, and *tar* for your system. VMS, DOS, and Mac versions are available. The VMS versions are on *gatekeeper.dec.com* in */archive/pub/VMS*.

Questions about BITFTP can be directed to Melinda Varian, *MAINT@PUCC* on BITNET.

UUCP

UUCP is standard on virtually all UNIX systems, and is available for IBM-compatible PCs and Apple Macintoshes. The examples are available by UUCP via modem from UUNET; UUNET's connect-time charges apply.

You can get the examples from UUNET whether you have an account or not. If you or your company has an account with UUNET, you will have a system with a direct UUCP connection to UUNET. Find that system, and type:

```
uucp uunet\!~/published/oreilly/nutshell/make/make.tar.Z yourhost\!~/yourname/
```

The backslashes can be omitted if you use the Bourne shell (*sh*) instead of *csh*. The file should appear some time later (up to a day or more) in the directory */usr/spool/uucppublic/yourname*. If you don't have an account but would like one so that you can get electronic mail, then contact UUNET at 703-204-8000.

It's a good idea to get the file */published/oreilly/nutshell/make/ls-lR.Z* as a short test file containing the filenames and sizes of all the files in the directory.

Once you've got the desired file, follow the directions under FTP to extract the files from the archive.

Conventions Used in This Handbook

The following conventions are used in this book:

Bold   is used to highlight new terms and concepts the first time they are introduced, options to commands, file suffixes such as **.c**, and C preprocessor directives.

Italic   is used to indicate files, directories, commands, and program names when they appear in the body of a paragraph. The string (1) after a name indicates a command that can be found in section 1 of a UNIX system's manual pages.

`Constant Width` is used in text to indicate constants and other strings from source files, including macros and variable names. `Constant width` is also used in examples to show the contents of files or the output from commands.

`Constant Bold`   is used in examples to show input that is typed literally by the user.

[]   surrounds optional elements in a description of program syntax in Appendix A. (The brackets themselves should never be typed.)

Acknowledgments

We wish to thank Tan Bronson and James Van Sciver for their thorough and well-informed suggestions. They helped us extract and clarify basic principles in some areas, and prodded us to add many new sections on advanced features. In particular, Tan warned us about the wealth of differences among *make* variants, and spent several extra weeks helping to develop and run tests that ferreted them out, particularly where VPATH is concerned. One of Jim's big contributions was to persuade us that automatic regeneration of header-file dependencies was an important issue, worthy of an example and extended discussion.

We also thank several readers for their corrections and suggestions for new material. In particular, Steven J. Richardson suggested that we show how macros can be used instead of suffix rules to define consistent sets of commands handling aggregates of files. Dennis Kowalski pointed out that the **–k** option always forces a successful exit code. Dave Cline pointed out additional inconsistencies in how VPATH works on different variants.

We'd Like to Hear From You

We have tested and verified all of the information in this book to the best of our ability, but you may find that features have changed (or even that we have made mistakes!). Please let us know about any errors you find, as well as your suggestions for future editions, by writing:

```
O'Reilly & Associates, Inc.
101 Morris Street
Sebastopol, CA 95472
1-800-998-9938 (in the US or Canada)
1-707-829-0515 (international/local)
1-707-829-0104 (FAX)
```

You can also send us messages electronically. To be put on the mailing list or request a catalog, send email to:

info@oreilly.com   (via the Internet)

To ask technical questions or comment on the book, send email to:

> *bookquestions@oreilly.com*   (via the Internet)

We have a web site for the book, where we'll list examples, errata, and any plans for future editions. You can access this page at:

> *http://www.oreilly.com/catalog/make2/*

For more information about this book and others, see the O'Reilly web site:

> *http://www.oreilly.com*

1

How to Write a Simple Makefile

The Description File
Dependency Checking
Minimizing Rebuilds
Invoking make
Basic Rules of Syntax

The command

```
$ make program
```

indicates that you want to "make" a version—usually the latest version—of *program*. Thus, if *program* is an executable file, your command indicates that you want to perform all necessary compilation and linking required to create the file. Instead of entering a great many *cc* compiler commands by hand, you use *make* to automate the process.

In discussing *make*, we call *program* the **target** of the operation. *program* is built from one or more files, called **prerequisites** or **dependents**. Each of these files may in turn have other files as prerequisites.

For instance, you build executable programs by linking object files. But if the source files or header files have changed, you probably want to recompile the object files before linking. Thus, each source file is the prerequisite for an object file.

The strength of *make* is its sensitivity to hierarchies of dependencies, such as source-to-object and object-to-executable. You are responsible for specifying some dependencies in a **description file**, which normally has the name *makefile* or *Makefile*. But *make* also understands its environment, and can determine many dependencies for itself. In deciding which files to build and how to build them, *make* draws on the names of existing files, the last-modified times of these files, and a set of built-in rules. With this background, a simple command like the previous one shown guarantees that all necessary parts of the hierarchy are updated.

The Description File

Suppose you are writing a program that consists of:

*   Three C language source files—*main.c, iodat.c, dorun.c.*

*   Assembly language code in *lo.s*, called by one of the C sources.

*   A set of library routines in */usr/fred/lib/crtn.a*.

If you built the program by hand, the complete set of commands would be:

```
$ cc -c main.c
$ cc -c iodat.c
$ cc -c dorun.c
$ as -o lo.o lo.s
$ cc -o program main.o iodat.o dorun.o lo.o /usr/fred/lib/crtn.a
```

Of course, you could compile, assemble, and link everything in one *cc* command, but in realistic programming environments this rarely happens. First, each source file might be built and tested separately, often by different people. Second, a major application can take hours to compile, so programmers commonly use existing object files whenever possible.

Now let us see how to specify commands to *make* through a description file. We create a file named *makefile* in the directory containing the source files, and type in the following contents. For the sake of illustration, this description file includes every command and dependency explicitly, although many of them are not required by *make*.

```
1    program :  main.o iodat.o dorun.o lo.o /usr/fred/lib/crtn.a
2         cc -o program main.o iodat.o dorun.o lo.o /usr/fred/lib/crtn.a

3    main.o :  main.c
4         cc -c main.c

5    iodat.o :  iodat.c
6         cc -c iodat.c

7    dorun.o :  dorun.c
8         cc -c dorun.c

9    lo.o :  lo.s
10        as -o lo.o lo.s
```

The numbers in the left margin are not part of the actual description file. They are shown here so that the explanation can refer to individual lines of the file conveniently.

This description file contains five entries. Each entry consists of a line containing a colon (the **dependency line** or **rules line**), and one or more **command lines** beginning with a tab. To the left of the colon on the dependency line is a target; to the right of the colon are the target's prerequisites. The tab-indented command lines, therefore, show how to build the targets out of their prerequisites.

In the description file shown here, line 1 says that *program* depends on the files *main.o, iodat.o, dorun.o,* and *lo.o,* as well as on the library */usr/fred/lib/crtn.a*. Line 2 specifies the compiler command that makes *program* from its prerequisites. (Since they are all object files or libraries, this command just invokes the linker.) Thus, assuming that *program* does not yet exist, you can enter the command

```
$ make program
```

and *make* executes the command on line 2. What if one of the object files does not exist either? You can build the missing file by passing it as an argument to *make*, but rarely is there a need to do so. The key contribution of *make* is its ability to decide on its own what has to be built.

Dependency Checking

When you ask *make* to build the *program* target, using the description file shown in the previous section, the command on line 2 does not execute right away. First, *make* checks to see whether a file named *program* exists. If so, *make* checks *main.o, iodat.o, dorun.o, lo.o,* and */usr/fred/lib/crtn.a* to see whether any of them are newer than *program*. This is easy to do because the operating system stores the time of last modification for every file—you can see the time by entering an *ls -l* command. If *program* was built since the latest modifications of all its prerequisites, *make* may decide that there is no need to rebuild it, and exit without issuing any commands.

But *make* has more work to do before reaching this decision. Each of the **.o** files must also be checked against its prerequisites. The succeeding entries in the description file provide the information necessary for this.

For example, line 3 shows that *main.o* depends on *main.c*. Thus, if *main.c* was modified after the last time *main.o* was made, *make* executes the compile command in line 4 and thus creates a new, up-to-date *main.o*. Only after all the subordinate prerequisites have been checked and all the prerequisites of *program* brought up to date, will *make* execute the command shown in line 2. Assuming that *main.c* is the only file that has changed since *program* was last built, the commands executed by *make* are

```
cc -c main.c
cc -o program main.o iodat.o dorun.o lo.o /usr/fred/lib/crtn.a
```

Since *make* echoes each command to the standard output before executing it, you can see the sequence of commands at your terminal after you invoke *make*.

In summary, program building consists of a chain of commands that must be issued in the correct order. You generally ask *make* to build the last file in that chain. Then *make* traces back through the chain of dependencies to find what commands must be executed. Finally, it moves forward through the chain, executing each command until your target is up to date. Thus, *make* is the most well-known example of a programming technique known as backward-chaining, which is usually restricted to relatively little-known environments like the Prolog language.

Minimizing Rebuilds

As a more complex example of how *make* can save you time and prevent confusion, consider a program that can exist in several different versions. Suppose you have written a data-plotting program that can be run either at a dumb terminal or a bit-mapped workstation. The bulk of the program involves calculations and file handling, and is identical in either version. You have stored all this code in a file named *basic.c*. The code that handles user input at a dumb terminal is in *prompt.c*, while the code that handles the bitmapped interface is in *window.c*.

Thus, the program can be released in two different versions, and you want to rebuild the appropriate version whenever you make a change. For the dumb terminal version, which you build from *basic.c* and *prompt.c*, you have decided to call the executable file *plot_prompt*. The bit-mapped version, which is built from *basic.c* and *window.c*, has the name *plot_win*. Here is a description file that handles both versions:

```
plot_prompt : basic.o prompt.o
     cc -o plot_prompt basic.o prompt.o

plot_win : basic.o window.o
     cc -o plot_win basic.o window.o

basic.o : basic.c
     cc -c basic.c

prompt.o : prompt.c
     cc -c prompt.c

window.o: window.c
     cc -c window.c
```

The first time you build one of the executable files, you have to compile *basic.c*. But so long as you never change that source file, and never delete *basic.o*, you never have to recompile it. If you change *prompt.c* and remake *plot_prompt*, *make* checks the modification times and realizes that it just needs to recompile *prompt.c* and relink. Here is the *make* command, and its results:

```
$ make plot_prompt
cc -c prompt.c
cc -o plot_prompt basic.o prompt.o
```

The description files in these examples could actually be simplified a great deal. The reason is that *make* has built-in rules and macro definitions to handle regularly occurring dependencies, such as the dependency of a **.o** file on a **.c** file. Chapter 2, *Macros*, and Chapter 3, *Suffix Rules*, discuss these features. In this chapter, we are interested just in conveying the concepts of dependency and updating.

Invoking make

The examples in the previous sections assume that:

• The project files, as well as the description files, reside in the same directory.

• The description files are named *makefile* or *Makefile*.

• The directory containing these files is the current directory when you enter the *make* command.

Given these conditions, you can build any target in the description file by entering the command

```
$ make target
```

Each command line required to build the target is echoed to your terminal and then executed. If some of the intermediate files exist and are up to date, *make* skips their commands. It executes only the minimal set of commands needed to rebuild *program*. If no prerequisite files were modified or removed since the last time *target* was created, *make* issues the message

```
`target´ is up to date
```

and does nothing else.

If you attempt to make a target that is not contained in the description file and not covered by the default rules discussed in Chapter 3, *Suffix Rules*, *make* will respond like this:

```
$ make nontarget
make:  Don't know how to make nontarget.  Stop.
```

or like this:

```
$ make nontarget
`nontarget´ is up to date.
```

The latter message appears if *nontarget* is a real file that actually exists in the current directory. Chapter 7, *Troubleshooting*, explains the different messages issued by *make* in various circumstances.

It is also possible to give *make* several targets in a single invocation. The effect is the same as issuing several *make* commands in succession.

```
$ make main.o dorun.o lo.o
```

Finally, you can simply type

```
$ make
```

with no target name. In this case, the first target contained in the description file is made (together, of course, with all its prerequisites).

make has many command-line options. For example, you can suppress echoing of command lines, or conversely, see what commands would be executed without actually executing them. These and other options are discussed in detail in Chapter 6, *Command-line Usage and Special Targets*.

Basic Rules of Syntax

Before you try to write your own description file, you should understand some of the subtle requirements that *make* imposes, which might not be clear from examples alone. A complete syntax description appears in Appendix A, *Quick Reference*; this section is just a set of hints for getting started.

The most important rule is to begin every command with a tab. An all-too-common error is to slip a space into the first column of a command. Naturally, casual inspection cannot distinguish spaces from tabs, and *make* unfortunately does not offer a very useful error message in such circumstances.

Since *make* recognizes a command by the initial tab, be sure *not* to start any other line with a tab. You will receive an error message if you use a tab as the first character of a dependency line, a comment, or even just a line of white space. Only the first character has this critical effect; tabs can be used freely anywhere else on the line.

If you want to check the tabs in your description file, issue the command,

```
$ cat -v -t -e makefile
```

where the **–v** and **–t** options cause all tabs to appear as ^I, and the **–e** option places a dollar sign at the end of each line so that you can see any terminating white space.

You can continue a long line by placing a backslash (\) at the end. Make sure the backslash is right before the newline; don't let any white space slip in between. A set of lines continued by backslashes is parsed as one line.

make ignores blank lines in description files. Likewise, it ignores characters from a pound sign (#) to the end of a line, so that # designates the beginning of a comment.

Commands need not occupy separate lines in the description file. You can place a command on a dependency line, preceded by a semicolon:

```
plot_prompt : prompt.o;  cc -o plot_prompt prompt.o
```

(This is the only exception to the rule that every command line in a description file must begin with a tab.)

A single target can appear on multiple dependency lines. This can be a useful practice when you are indicating different kinds of dependencies:

```
file.o : /usr/src/file.c
    cc -c /usr/src/file.c
    .
    .
    .
file.o : global.h defs.h
```

The command that actually creates *file.o* lies under the first dependency line. But even if */usr/src/file.c* doesn't change, *make* can see that *file.o* is out of date and recompile it, if either **.h** file changes.

If you use multiple dependency lines, only one of them can be associated with commands. An exception to this rule involves a dependency line with two colons, a special syntax that is useful for building libraries and is discussed in Chapter 3, *Suffix Rules*.

Finally, you can have targets without prerequisites. (The colon, however, must be present.) Many of these targets aren't even filenames. For instance, many description files contain the following target, to help the programmer remove temporary files after a busy day testing programs:

```
clean:
    /bin/rm -f core *.o
```

The command

```
$ make clean
```

will inevitably result in execution of the command script shown in the entry, as long as there is not an actual file named *clean*. This is because *make* treats every non-existent target as an out-of-date target.

The commands in your entries, for now, should be just single-line Bourne shell commands. Until you read Chapter 4, *Commands*, do not try to use aliases, environment variables, or multi-line commands like *if* and *for*. Also avoid *cd*, for reasons explained in Chapter 4.

You should now be able to create your own description files simply by entering the commands you are used to typing at the terminal. Soon, however, you will start to find this tedious. The next two chapters explain the many ways in which you can simplify and generalize your description files.

2

Macros

Syntax Rules
Internally Defined Macros
Macro Definitions on the Command Line
Shell Variables
Priority of Macro Assignments
Relying on Environment Variables for
    Defaults
Macro String Substitution
Internal Macros for Prerequisites and
    Targets

The description files in the last chapter contain a lot of repetition. You can easily imagine that in a real project, where targets can depend on dozens of files and can be built in several different versions, the amount of repeated text could be overwhelming. But most real-life description files are actually succinct—10 to 50 short lines. This is possible because of two powerful features in *make*: macros and suffix rules. We discuss macros in this chapter, and suffix rules in Chapter 3.

Description file entries of the form

```
name = text string
```

are macro definitions. Subsequent references to

```
$(name)
```

or

```
${name}
```

are interpreted as

```
text string
```

These, for instance, are all valid macro definitions:

```
LIBES = -lX11
objs = drawable.o plot_points.o root_data.o
CC=/usr/fred/bin/cc
23 = "This is the (23)rd run"
OPT =
DEBUG_FLAG =     # empty now, but assign -g for debugging
BINDIR = /usr/local/bin
```

An entry in the same description file might look like this:

```
plot : ${objs}
    ${CC} -o plot ${DEBUG_FLAG} ${objs} ${LIBES}
    mv plot ${BINDIR}
```

When you invoke *make plot*, the command evaluates to:

```
/usr/fred/bin/cc -o plot  drawable.o plot_points.o root_data.o -lX11
mv plot /usr/local/bin
```

This brief example reveals the main reasons for using macros. First, you can refer conveniently to files or command options that appear repeatedly in the description file. In this example, **objs** refers to the object files from which *plot* is built, and LIBES to a directory of libraries. Macros make it easier to change the description file without introducing inconsistencies.

Second, macros permit variations from one build to the next. In this example, DEBUG_FLAG controls whether the compiler creates symbolic information for the debugger.

Directories are especially common in macros. A macro like BINDIR above is valuable both for repetition and for variations in builds.

Syntax Rules

A macro definition is a line containing an equal sign. *make* associates the name (a sequence of letters and digits) to the left of the equal sign with the string of characters following it. You don't need to delimit the string with double or single quotes. If you do, as in the definition of **23** above, the quotes are preserved as part of the string.

A pound sign (#) ends the definition and starts a comment, as in any other line of a description file. Both the macro and its definition can be quite long. You can use a backslash at the end of a line to indicate that it continues on the following line. To ensure that *make* can distinguish a macro definition from a command or a dependency line, no tabs are permitted before the macro name, and no colons before the equal sign.

Since the ultimate disposition of every string in *make* is its use in a shell command, white space is handled rather casually. Blanks and tabs immediately to the left and right of the equal sign are stripped off. When you use a backslash to continue a line, *make* automatically substitutes one space. All further spaces, tabs, and newlines around the backslash are reduced to a single space. Other than these special places, *make* preserves all the spaces and tabs embedded within the string.

Macro names, by convention, are in uppercase. As the previous section showed, you can use any combination you want of uppercase and lowercase letters, digits, and underlines. Other punctuation characters sometimes work too, but we recommend that you avoid them. It is hard to predict which ones *make* can parse correctly. In particular, avoid shell metacharacters like \ and >.

When you refer to a macro—that is, when you want *make* to replace it with its definition—enclose the macro either in parentheses or in curly braces, and precede it with a dollar sign. In this book, we use curly braces, because parentheses have another meaning in relation to libraries (a subject discussed in Chapter 3, *Suffix Rules*).

Single-character macro names do not require either parentheses or braces, although it is a good habit to use them. In the case of the macro definition,

```
A = XYZ
```

the references $A, $(A), and ${A} are identical.

It is permissible to include macros in macro definitions, as in

```
ABC = XYZ
FILE = TEXT.${ABC}
```

References to ${FILE} will then evaluate to TEXT.XYZ.

A macro definition that has no string after the equal sign (like OPT and DEBUG_FLAG above), is assigned the null string. Thus, in the example above, *make* builds the *cc* command line as if the ${DEBUG_FLAG} reference were not there.

In addition, if you refer to a macro without defining it, *make* substitutes a null string. Thus, you will never get an error message for undefined macros.

You don't have to worry about the order in which you define macros. This makes it easy to nest definitions (although *make* quite correctly quits and complains if you define a macro recursively):

```
SOURCES    = ${MY_SRC} ${SHARED_SRC}
MY_SRC     = parse.c search_file.c
SHARED_DIR = /users/b_proj/src
SHARED_SRC = ${SHARED_DIR}/depend.c
```

No matter in which order you list the above definitions, ${SOURCES} evaluates to

```
parse.c search_file.c /users/b_proj/src/depend.c
```

(There is, however, one restriction: a macro must be defined before any dependency line in which it appears.)

This freedom of ordering implies a limitation. You cannot define a macro one way for part of a file and then redefine it. *make* simply uses the last definition in the file for all references, before and after. If you want to redefine macros dynamically, you have to invoke *make* recursively, a topic we discuss in Chapter 5, *Project Management*.

Internally Defined Macros

make predefines a number of common commands as macros. For instance, the ${CC} macro is always recognized by *make* as the C compiler, and the ${LD} macro as the linker. The main advantages of these predefined macros lie in their use with suffix rules, which we explain in Chapter 3, *Suffix Rules*. But it is helpful for you to know that if you see a description file like this:

```
basic.o : basic.c
    ${CC} -c basic.c
```

the effect is normally the same as if it were written like this:

```
basic.o : basic.c
    cc -c basic.c
```

If you look back at the first example in this chapter, you see that someone redefined CC so that it evaluated to */usr/fred/bin/cc*. You often find this kind of playing around with macros in development environments that are volatile, where common utilities like the C compiler are undergoing change. Presumably, */usr/fred/bin/cc* is someone's personal version of the compiler. Although most programmers don't have to worry about the stability of their compiler, the example shows how you can use *make* macros to support work by different people under a variety of conditions.

For each command that *make* defines as a macro, another macro is defined to hold command options. Programmers generally store their options to the C compiler in CFLAGS, options to *ld* in LDFLAGS, and so on. These are discussed in Chapter 3, *Suffix Rules*, because they are more relevant to the discussion of suffix rules.

Chapter 3 also explains how you can display all internally defined macros using the **-p** option to *make*.

Macro Definitions on the Command Line

You can define macros on the *make* command line. The following invocation:

```
$ make jgref DIR=/usr/proj
```

assigns the string `/usr/proj` to the name DIR; the description file then has access to the string as `${DIR}`. Usually you find targets before macro definitions on a command line, but the order is really irrelevant. This is because the equal sign marks an argument as a macro definition.

If the definition on your command line consists of several words, enclose them in double or single quotes. This is simply a matter of shell syntax. The quotes ensure that the shell passes the macro definition to *make* as a single argument. For example:

```
$ make jgref "DIR=/usr/proj /usr/lib /usr/proj/lib"
```

Finally, in the Bourne and Korn shells, you can define the macro before the *make* command:

```
$ DIR=/usr/proj make jgref
```

The order makes a slight difference in whether *make* can override the shell's definitions. We discuss the order later in this chapter.

Shell Variables

Shell variables that are part of the environment when you invoke *make* are available as macros within description files. However, you must refer to them using parentheses or curly braces (as described in the preceding section) whenever their names contain more than one character. Therefore, if you type a variable definition to the shell before invoking *make*:

```
$ DIR=/usr/proj; export DIR
$ make jgref
```

then you can use DIR in your description file:

```
SRC = ${DIR}/src

jgref :
    cd ${DIR}; ...
```

The commands shown above work in both the Bourne shell and the Korn shell. C shell users can add shell variables to the environment with the **setenv** command:

```
% setenv DIR /usr/proj
```

Thus, any environment variables you set in your *.profile* or *.login* file—or by any other means—are available within description files.

Note the difference between these environment variables, which are available as macros, and the limited possibility for use of dynamically assigned shell variables we discuss at the end of Chapter 4, *Commands*. The latter require a double dollar sign ($$), can appear without curly braces or parentheses, and are ineffectual across newlines.

Priority of Macro Assignments

We have already seen that there are several sources for the macros referred to within description files: the current shell environment, command-line definitions, *make* defaults, and the description file itself. If a macro is given conflicting definitions from different sources, which definition does *make* choose? That is, if DIR is defined to be /usr/proj in the description file, but is defined as /usr/proj/lib in the current shell environment, which definition does *make* actually use? Here is the order of priority, from least to greatest:

1. Internal (default) definitions of *make*.

2. Current shell environment variables. This includes macros that you enter on the *make* command line, if they precede the *make* command itself (Bourne and Korn shell only).

3. Description file macro definitions.

4. Macros that you enter on the *make* command line, if they follow the *make* command itself.

Thus, the description file ultimately determines what happens when you invoke *make*. What you see in the file will not be overridden by the relatively hidden shell environment or the default definitions, but only by what you yourself type on the *make* command line.

The low priority of environment variables is usually desirable, because project teams want a consistent development environment for different users. However, there may be circumstances in which you would like the environment to override the description file. For instance, suppose that you want to replace several of your project's default definitions with your own, and you have to run *make* over and over. The easiest solution is to define the macros in your environment and force it to override the description file. Invoke *make* with the –e option, which institutes the following order of priority from least to greatest:

1. Internal (default) definitions of *make*.

2. Description file macro definitions.

3. Current shell environment variables. This includes macros that you enter on the *make* command line, if they precede the *make* command itself (Bourne and Korn shell only).

4. Macros that you enter on the *make* command line, if they follow the *make* command itself.

Here is an example. The description file entry is:

```
TESTER = default_test
test : srcfile.c
    ${TESTER} srcfile.c
```

while you also define TESTER as an environment variable:

```
$ TESTER=new_test
$ export TESTER
```

The following command ignores your environment variable and uses the definition in the description file:

```
$ make test
default_test srcfile.c
```

But this command uses your environment variables:

```
$ make -e test
new_test srcfile.c
```

Relying on Environment Variables for Defaults

Environment variables are a traditional—and perhaps a greatly overused—way to handle differences between systems or users. For instance, if one vendor or system adminstrator wants software tools to be installed in */usr/local* while another prefers */usr/share*, toolsmiths can keep them both happy by inserting a variable into all pathnames and telling users to define it properly for their systems.

Since *make* treats environment variables as macros, you can use the same technique in your builds. Many people also like to use environment variables when they have to execute recursive makes, as shown in Chapter 5, *Project Management*. It's more convenient to use an environment variable than to pass a macro definition on every *make* command line.

Here are some sample macro definitions and an entry from a description file, generalized to use an environment variable. The example assumes that you keep your local utilities in a directory called *tool* somewhere on every system. The particular utility used in this example has the unexciting name of *filter*.

```
TOOL_DIR = ${PROJECT_TREE}/tool

FILTER = ${TOOL_DIR}/filter

source_stream:
        cat *.c | ${FILTER} ...
```

The key to maintaining independence is that everything in the file rests on PROJECT_TREE as the root directory, but nowhere in the file is PROJECT_TREE defined. That must be done by each user. Thus, on systems where the *tool* directory lies in */usr/local*, users put this in their *.profile* files (Bourne or Korn shell):

```
PROJECT_TREE=/usr/local ; export PROJECT_TREE
```

or this in their *.cshrc* files (C shell):

```
setenv PROJECT_TREE /usr/local
```

This definition is then propagated throughout the description file, setting TOOL_DIR and FILTER properly, and leading to the command:

```
cat *.c | /usr/local/tool/filter ...
```

If you defined PROJECT_TREE in the description file, anyone who happened to have a different root directory would be greatly inconvenienced. These users would have to override your choice on every *make* command line, either by defining PROJECT_TREE or by using the –e option.

Leaving PROJECT_TREE undefined is much more flexible—so long as users make sure to define the environment variable. What if they don't? Then there is trouble—that is the great weakness of environment variables. In this particular case, the PROJECT_TREE macro resolves to a null string. So the description file tries to run a utility named */tool/filter*, which does not exist, and the build is quickly derailed. The user probably has no idea what went wrong, so several people on the team can get dragged in and waste a lot of time debugging a simple problem.

Incidentally, if you put the following line in a description file, it does not mean that PROJECT_TREE is undefined.

```
PROJECT_TREE =
```

This defines PROJECT_TREE to be a null string, a definition that overrides an environment variable.

Perhaps what you want to do is set a default that suits most users, while allowing them to change it easily if they need to. Thus, if the root is */usr/local* on most systems, you can take care of the definition, and users never have to worry about it. On systems that differ, users can set an environment variable in *.profile .cshrc*, and your description file respects that.

Surprise! You cannot do this in *make*. You can leave a macro undefined, or you can define it and make it hard to change. To really support the notion of a default, you have to go outside *make* and use a shell script.

An example of such a shell script—often called a wrapper—appears below. The script checks to see whether the user has defined PROJECT_TREE. If so, the script leaves it alone. Otherwise, PROJECT_TREE takes your chosen default. The last line invokes *make*, passing all the arguments from the command line.

```
if
   test -z "$PROJECT_TREE"
then
   PROJECT_TREE=usr/local ; export PROJECT_TREE
fi

make $*
```

Now you must train all your users to invoke the script instead of *make*. For instance, if you call it *make_local*, they have to enter:

```
$ make_local source_stream
```

The whole process appears very round-about, but most of the time it works. The most likely source of trouble is complicated command arguments; for instance, quotes get stripped off of arguments and are never seen by the final *make* command.

Like environment variables, you should use wrapper scripts as a last resort, because they raise new problems when solving old ones. For instance, there is one utility that you can never locate using the example in this section—the *make_local* script itself!

Macro String Substitution

(This feature is not available in all variants of *make;* see Appendix C for a way to check your system.) Suppose you have the macro definition,

```
SRCS = defs.c redraw.c calc.c
```

The description file command,

```
ls ${SRCS:.c=.o}
```

then produces the output,

```
calc.o    defs.o    redraw.o
```

assuming these files exist. While the macro reference has a rather difficult syntax, the effect is simple. *make* evaluates `${SRCS}`, searches for the string following the colon, and substitutes the string following the equal sign. This makes it easy to maintain groups of files that differ only in their suffix, or in their trailing characters. For instance:

```
SRCS = defs.c redraw.c calc.c
FINAL_OBJS = ${SRCS:.c=.o}
DEBUG_OBJS = ${SRCS:.c=_dbg.o}
```

If you add or remove a source file later, you need to change only the SRCS macro definition. `${FINAL_OBJS}` evaluates to

```
defs.o redraw.o calc.o
```

while `${DEBUG_OBJS}` evaluates to

```
defs_dbg.o redraw_dbg.o calc_dbg.o
```

If you want to build an executable purely from `${DEBUG_OBJS}`, you can use an entry like this:

```
plot_debug: ${DEBUG_OBJS}
        ${CC} -o plot_debug ${DEBUG_OBJS}
```

String substitution is severely restricted; can take place only at the end of the macro, or immediately before white space. That is, the description file entry,

```
LETTERS = xyz xyzabc abcxyz
...
        echo ${LETTERS:xyz=DEF}
```

produces the output,

```
DEF xyzabc abcDEF
```

because the `abc` masks the presence of the second `xyz`.

The second string in a substitution can be null, but not the first. Thus, given

```
SOURCES = src1.c src2.c glob.c
EXECS = ${SOURCES:.c=}
```

`${EXECS}` evaluates to

```
src1 src2 glob
```

Other, more powerful, forms of macro string substitution are available in some versions of *make*. These vary greatly; check the documentation for your version. The general practice is to let a percent sign (%) match any string.

There clearly are many times when you would like to define a single set of commands that work for many types of files. Compiling a **.c** file to create an **.o** file is an obvious example. Chapter 3, *Suffix Rules*, introduces the general solution used in *make*. But you might still find macros and string substitution useful for recognizing and handling other patterns besides suffixes; for instance, the *_dbg.o* pattern shown earlier in this section.

Internal Macros for Prerequisites and Targets

make defines several macros of its own each time it reads a dependency line. These can simplify your description files and make it easier to add and change entries. The most common of the macros are defined here. Appendix A, *Quick Reference*, lists all of them.

The `$@` macro evaluates to the current target. This macro is quite common in description files, because the target is usually the name of a file you are trying to build. Thus, an entry compiling an executable program generally uses @ as the name of the output file:

```
plot_prompt : basic.o prompt.o
    cc -o $@ basic.o prompt.o
```

The $? macro evaluates to a list of prerequisites that are newer than the current target. For instance, suppose you have a library named *libops* containing three object files, *interact.o*, *sched.o*, and *gen.o*. The following description entry rebuilds the library with any object files that are newer than the library itself:

```
libops : interact.o sched.o gen.o
    ar r $@ $?
```

The first time you build *libops*, all the object modules are put in, because *make* always considers a non-existent target to be out of date.

```
$ make libops
ar r libops interact.o sched.o gen.o
```

Later, if you recompile *sched.o*, that module is the only one replaced in the library:

```
$ cc -c sched.c
$ make libops
ar r libops sched.o
```

Chapter 3, *Suffixes*, discusses libraries in detail.

A single entry in your description file can run multiple times with different targets and prerequisites. For instance, suppose the entry is:

```
new_spec new_impl : menus hash store
    date >> $@
    ls $? >> $@
```

If someone on your team changed *menus* and rebuilt *new_impl* yesterday, and then somebody changed *store* today, both *menus* and *store* are newer than *new_spec*. But *store* is the only prerequisite newer than *new_impl*. Now rebuild both targets:

```
$ make new_spec
date >> new_spec
ls menus store >> new_spec
$ make new_impl
date >> new_impl
ls store >> new_impl
```

Another variation of $@ is $$@, with two dollar signs. (This feature is not available in all variants of *make*; see Appendix C for a way to check your system.) This macro is meaningful only on dependency lines—that is, it can be used only in specifying a prerequisite. In contrast, $? and $@ can be used only on command lines.

$$@ refers to exactly the same thing as $@—namely, the current target. The double dollar sign is necessary because of the order in which *make* reads and interprets lines in the description file. Thus, the dependency line

```
docmk : $$@.c
```

evaluates to

```
docmk : docmk.c
```

This is useful for building large numbers of executable files, each of which has only one source file. For instance, the source directories for building UNIX system commands sometimes contain description files like this:

```
CMDS = cat dd echo date cc cmp comm ar ld chown
${CMDS} : $$@.c
        ${CC} -O $? -o $@
```

Typing the command,

```
$ make echo
```

then becomes the same as if you had the description file entry:

```
echo : echo.c
        cc -O echo.c -o echo
```

Similarly, if you type

```
$ make cat date cmp ar
```

make builds each target in turn, with $$@ evaluating to *cat* while *cat* is the target, to *date* while *date* is the target, and so on.

By the way, syntax rules for single-character macros apply to the ones in this section. So if you want, you can write $(@) or ${@} for $@.

There are additional internal macros not described here, as well as ways to extract the filename part or directory part of a macro. You will encounter these features in Chapter 3 and Chapter 5. Appendix A contains a list of all internal macros and available transformations.

In light of all this, our first description file from Chapter 1, *How to Write a Simple Makefile*, can become much shorter, although a little hard to read:

```
OBJS = main.o iodat.o dorun.o lo.o
LIB = /usr/proj/lib/crtn.a

program : ${OBJS} ${LIB}
    ${CC} -o $@ ${OBJS} ${LIB}

main.o : main.c
    ${CC} -c $?

iodat.o : iodat.c
    ${CC} -c $?

dorun.o : dorun.c
    ${CC} -c $?

lo.o : lo.s
    ${AS} -o $@ $?
```

You might think that the *cc* command that builds *program* could have specified
$? in the place of ${OBJS}. However, $? represents only those prerequisite
files that are more recently modified than the target, whereas the *cc* command
must link together *all* the object modules comprising the program.

The last four entries in the file still show a lot of repetition, and it would appear
that adding or removing any source files from the program calls for careful maintenance work on the description file. For variants of *make* that support string substitution, you could generalize all entries referring to .c files:

```
C_OBJS = main.o iodat.o dorun.o

${C_OBJS} : $${@:.o=.c}
    ${CC} -c $?
```

But *make* provides a cleaner solution for handling files in aggregates. In the next
chapter, you will see how suffix rules automate and greatly reduce the work of
writing a description file.

3

Suffix Rules

What is a Suffix Rule?
Commands Supported by Default Suffix
Rules
How to Display Defaults
Writing Your Own Suffix Rules

Even the simplified description file at the end of the last chapter can be reduced further. Most of the activities that it describes—compiling and assembling—are governed by certain conventions, and therefore can be carried out by *make* under a set of default rules.

On UNIX systems, C language source files always have a **.c** suffix—a requirement imposed by the *cc* compiler. Similarly, Fortran source files have a **.f** suffix, and assembly language source files have a **.s** suffix. Furthermore, the C and Fortran compilers automatically place object modules into **.o** files.

Such conventions make it possible for *make* to do many tasks by acting upon a set of **suffix rules**. Relying upon these rules, we can simplify our sample description file to the following:

```
OBJS = main.o iodat.o dorun.o lo.o
LIB = /usr/proj/lib/crtn.a

program  :  ${OBJS} ${LIB}
    ${CC} -o $@ ${OBJS} ${LIB}
```

While building *program, make* first checks to see whether *main.o* is up to date. It does this by looking for any file in the current directory that, according to standard suffix rules, could be used to make *main.o*. If it finds a file, *main.c*, and if that file has been changed since *main.o* was last made, *make* applies one of its rules by invoking the C compiler on *main.c*. Or if *make* finds a file, *main.f*, that is more recent than *main.o*, it invokes the Fortran compiler. The search proceeds similarly with the assembler and **.s** files.

For our sample description file, the default rules are sufficient to perform all the updating tasks except the final *cc* command that links together the objects and the library. The description file recognizes not only

```
$ make program
```

but also

```
$ make iodat.o
```

and so on, since the subordinate targets are also covered by default rules.

By knowing the default suffix rules, or by defining your own suffix rules, you can greatly reduce the complexity of your description files.

What is a Suffix Rule?

In effect, suffix rules amount to predefined, generalized description file entries. Here are the precise definitions of the rules our example draws upon:

```
.SUFFIXES  :  .o .c .s

.c.o :
    $(CC) $(CFLAGS) -c $<
.s.o :
    $(AS) $(ASFLAGS) -o $@ $<
```

(We'll explain the meaning of the $< macro shortly.)

The macros used in the commands all receive default definitions, as described in Chapter 2, *Macros*, although you can override them. The .SUFFIXES line has the form of a dependency line, but with a difference. The strings on this line represent the suffixes that *make* will consider significant. If a prerequisite ends in one of these suffixes, but has no explicit, user-supplied commands associated with it, *make* looks for an applicable suffix rule. Consider, for example, our simplified description file. When building *program*, *make* performs the following steps:

1. Look at each of the prerequisite files given by ${OBJS} and ${LIB}, and treat each of these files as a target in turn. That is, see whether any of the prerequisite files needs to be made before *program* is made. Remember, while *make* works from the top (original target) downward in determining the

hierarchy of prerequisites, it always works from the bottom upward in actually modifying, or making, targets.

2. *program* depends on *iodat.o*, among other files. When looking at *iodat.o* dependencies, *make* checks first for a user-specified dependency line containing *iodat.o* as a target. Finding none, it notes that the **.o** suffix is significant, and therefore looks for another file in the current directory that can be used to make *iodat.o*. Such a file must:

   — Have the same name (apart from suffix) as *iodat.o*.

   — Have a significant suffix.

   — Be able to be used in order to make *iodat.o* according to an existing suffix rule.

   In this case *iodat.c* meets all the requirements. The suffix rule we need was given above, and is one of the default rules of *make*:

```
.c.o :
        $(CC) $(CFLAGS) -c $<
```

   This rule describes how to make a **.o** file from a **.c** file. The syntax is similar to, but not quite the same as, regular description file entries. Here $< has a meaning akin to $?, except that $< can be used only in suffix rules. It evaluates to whatever prerequisite triggered the rule—that is, to *iodat.c*. The **.o** file can be considered the target of this rule, and the **.c** file the prerequisite.

3. *make* goes ahead and executes the suffix rule for creating a new *iodat.o* only if:

   — There are no further prerequisites that must be checked out first. (Does *iodat.c* depend on any other files, either explicitly or according to suffix rules? The answer is no.)

   — *iodat.o* is actually outdated with respect to *iodat.c*.

4. Finally, after going through this process for each file in ${OBJS} and ${LIB}, *make* executes the *ld* command to recreate *program* only if *program* was out of date with respect to any files in its hierarchy of prerequisites.

Command Options

The previous examples contained macros named **CFLAGS** and **ASFLAGS**. Related macros are defined by *make* for practically every utility it invokes in its suffix rules. As the names suggest, these macros let you pass flags—or options, as they are usually called in modern documentation—to the commands.

For instance, if you want to debug your program, you want *make* to compile all your programs with the **–g** option. The **CFLAGS** macro provides the hook that lets you communicate your intention to *make*. Just set **CFLAGS** in your command line:

```
$ make program CFLAGS=-g
```

or set it explicitly in your description file:

```
OBJS = main.o iodat.o dorun.o lo.o
CFLAGS = -g
```

and the option will be passed to each *cc* command, resulting in execution of the following:

```
cc -g -c main.c
cc -g -c iodat.c
    ...
```

If you want to pass multiple options in a single macro on the *make* command line, enclose the whole definition in double quotes. For instance, the following commands change the suffix rules so that they compile all C files with **–g** and **–DTRACE**:

```
$ make program "CFLAGS=-g -DTRACE"
```

Your specified **CFLAGS** overrides the default **CFLAGS** defined by *make*, which is **–O**. This is fine for these particular options, since you usually don't want to optimize when debugging. Chapter 5, *Project Management*, shows how to preserve default options while adding one of your own.

CFLAGS, and the related macros provided for other utilities, always appear just after the name of the command. This is reasonable for most options because they should precede the list of filenames. But one critical exception exists: the **–l** option that passes library names to the linker.

The **–l** option has to follow the filenames in the *cc* or *ld* command. Therefore, do not try to pass it in **CFLAGS**. Use a separate macro, for instance:

```
BASICLIBRARIES= -lX11 -lm

plot : ${OBJS}
        ${CC} ${CFLAGS} -o $@ ${OBJS} ${BASICLIBRARIES}
```

In some variants of *make*, the suffix rules for compilations provide a built-in macro where you can specify libraries; look for this macro in the documentation or in the **–p** output described later in this chapter.

Command options can lead to a pitfall in which the greatest strength of *make* becomes a trap. Suppose you change the library options in a description file entry and then invoke *make* upon the targets. If up-to-date targets already exist, *make* will not rebuild them. For example, if you previously created *iodat.o* with different command options and have not changed *iodat.c* since then, *make* will just compile the other files and link them with the old *iodat.o*. This will lead to error messages from the linker or very confusing results at run time.

After all, *make* gets information only from filenames and modification times. Nothing can tell it what options were used to create a target. Chapter 5 and Appendix B discuss some of the workarounds and enhancements designed to overcome this gap in information.

Internal Macros

We have just seen that $<, used in suffix rule commands, yields the name of the prerequisite that is being used to make the *target*—for example, the **.c** file in a **.c.o** rule. Another macro available only in suffix rule commands is $*, representing the filename part (without suffix) of the prerequisite. The suffix rule command,

```
cp $< $*.tmp
```

therefore evaluates to

```
cp main.c main.tmp
```

if *main.c* is the prerequisite the rule is acting upon.

Chapter 2 introduced the $? macro, which evaluates to a list of prerequisites that are newer than the target. Conceptually, this is quite close to the $< macro. But traditionally, *make* has kept them separate, allowing $< only in suffix rules, and $? only in normal entries that contain targets and prerequisites. Some newer versions of *make* allow $? in suffix rules, where its meaning is the same as $<, but to keep description files portable you should stick to $< in suffix rules.

Commands Supported by Default Suffix Rules

The rules built into *make* reflect the popular compilers and programming tools that were available on UNIX systems when *make* was developed. Luckily (for you as a novice *make* user, if not for the field of software engineering as a whole) the utilities and practices employed by C programmers have remained the same.

Thus, to build a **.o** file, *make* starts by looking for a **.c** file and, if one exists, runs it through the C compiler. Otherwise (focusing on just the C environment for a moment), *make* looks for a **.y** file on which it can run *yacc*, and if that fails, a **.l** file on which it can run *lex*.

When we look beyond C programming, the default rules have not stood up so well over time. That is why it's a good thing that you can redefine the rules, as described later in this chapter.

Fortran and Pascal

Fortran compilers have changed a great deal from the days of early UNIX systems. Some implementations have changed the default suffix rules to match the utilities on their systems, while others have not.

For instance, some implementations of *make* still look for *fc* as the compiler, instead of the modern *f77*. That is easy enough to fix by defining this in your shell environment or description file:

```
FC=f77
```

Most implementations still do not recognize the uppercase **.F** suffix (for Fortran files that pass through the C preprocessor). You can fix this by copying the **.f** rules, and adding **.F** to the **.SUFFIXES** list. (This procedure will be clear later, when we explain how to write your own suffix rules.)

```
.SUFFIXES: .F

.F.o:
     $(FC) $(FFLAGS) -c $<
     .
     .
     .
```

Meanwhile, the odds are good that your *make* recognizes **.r** and **.e** suffixes, which correspond to the obsolete Ratfor and EFL preprocessors that were used before the advent of Fortran 77. These rules do no harm, but they are strange relics, and it will be interesting to see when they finally disappear from released versions of *make*.

Pass options to the Fortran compiler through FFLAGS.

If your system offers a Pascal compiler, it almost certainly also offers the corresponding suffix rules in *make*. They probably look like this:

```
.p.o:
    $(PC) $(PFLAGS) -c $<
    .
    .
    .
```

Given this rule, you can pass options to the Pascal compiler through PFLAGS.

SCCS and RCS

The most restrictive effects of outdated default rules can be found in *make*'s limited support for SCCS (Source Code Control System). This utility keeps backup versions of source files to help project teams maintain multiple versions and recover from unwanted changes or accidental file corruption. While competing tools have emerged to perform this critical function, SCCS is still the most common on UNIX systems. RCS (Revision Control System, a free software product) is becoming a close contender.

In the view taken by *make*, a source control file is just another prerequisite in the chain of dependencies. For instance, if you are trying to build a .o file and no source file exists, *make* tries to create a source file by searching for an SCCS file and then, if successful, executing a *get* command.

Support for SCCS had to be built into *make* in a different manner from other rules, because SCCS is unique in its naming conventions: it manages files by prefixes rather than suffixes. To maintain a backup version of a file, SCCS creates a new file consisting of the prefix s. followed by the filename. Thus, when you place a C language source file named *filename.c* under SCCS control, it creates a file with the name *s.filename.c*.

Unfortunately, two different interfaces to SCCS exist, one distributed by AT&T and one by U.C. Berkeley, but System V *make* works only with the older—and less popular—one. The AT&T interface is distinguished by keeping backup versions in the same directory as working source files. The Berkeley interface is a front-end to the AT&T one, and maintains the backup version of each working file in a subdirectory that has the name SCCS.

Do you want to mix source control and builds?

Nowadays, large team projects tend to keep source control separate from compilation and building. They find it easier to write separate tools invoking SCCS or RCS, and not to use the support within *make* at all. One reason is that source files are scattered among many directories, and the SCCS or RCS files reside on hub systems instead of with the programmers' working files. This makes it extremely hard for *make* to find the files during dependency checks.

A more fundamental reason for placing a wall between source control and the build process is that automatic updating may be undesirable. Imagine that you have gotten and changed some of your team's files in order to fix a bug. While editing and testing, you need a stable set of files; you do not want *make* to substitute a new version that someone else has placed into SCCS or RCS. The safe strategy is to prevent automatic updating by *make*, and to put the responsibility on the programmer for getting all the correct files before each build.

Certainly, you can create *make* entries to get and return files from the source control directories, just as you can use *make* for other general tasks. But when other people are sharing an SCCS or RCS tree with you, you should not let *make* update your source files automatically.

Automatic gets or check-outs can be very convenient if you are working on a project by yourself. So let us continue and see what *make* offers.

The tilde (˜) convention

Suffix rules use tildes to identify SCCS files. For example, the default suffix rule,

```
.c˜.o :
    $(GET) $(GFLAGS) -p $< > $*.c
    $(CC) $(CFLAGS) -c $*.c
    rm -f $*.c
```

describes how to transform a C language source file under SCCS control into an object file. The first half (.c˜) of the suffix pair represents a file of the form *s.filename.c*, from which *make* builds *filename.c* and *filename.o*. Thus, if we have a file *s.filename.c* in the current directory, the command

```
$ make filename.o
```

results in the execution of these commands:

```
get -p s.filename.c > filename.c
cc -O -c filename.c
rm -f filename.c
```

This special use of the tilde in *make* should not be confused with other conventional uses for a tilde, such as in backup versions of Emacs files or home directories in the C Shell. Similarly, *make* assigns this meaning to the tilde only in the dependency lines used for .SUFFIXES and suffix rules. If you see the following command in a description file:

```
rm -f *~
```

it means just what it appears to mean—remove all files ending with a tilde.

The tilde convention is a rather makeshift one, designed to avoid changing the syntax of suffix rule lines to accommodate SCCS files. *make* is sophisticated enough to look in the current directory for *s.filename.c*, but nowhere else. Luckily, some implementations of *make* have been extended to look for an *SCCS* directory, so that they work with the Berkeley front-end. Using the VPATH feature discussed in Chapter 5, *Project Management*, you can induce the same behavior. Just put in your description file:

```
VPATH = SCCS
```

If the relationship between your build directory and your source control directory gets any more complicated—as it does on many large projects involving multiple directories—you will probably be frustrated by any attempt to use the built-in SCCS support in *make*. You can try some of the techniques for multiple directories and distributed files in Chapter 5, *Project Management*. But as you try to build in more and more sophisticated uses for the source control commands, you will find that *make* is just too unwieldy.

The $* macro has been slightly adapted to fit SCCS conventions. Take a simple case where *make* searches for a way to build *filename.c*, and succeeds in finding *s.filename.c*. The internal suffix rule *make* uses is:

```
.c~.c :
        $(GET) $(GFLAGS) -p $< > $*.c
```

If you tried to apply suffix rules strictly, you would insist that $* evaluate to *s.filename*. To make the macro useful, however, *make* strips off both the s. prefix and the .c suffix. So $* evaluates to *filename*, and the command

```
$(GET) $(GFLAGS) -p $< > $*.c
```

evaluates to

```
get -p s.filename.c > filename.c
```

The *get* command invoked by a suffix rule retrieves the most recent revision (delta) of a file. You can theoretically use GFLAGS to specify an earlier revision. But this is not easy to do in practice, because the numbers tend to change, and because you might find that you want a different revision number for each file.

Types of source files supported

For every kind of default suffix rule involving a source file—**.f** (Fortran files), **.y** (*yacc* files), **.s** (assembly language files), and so on—*make* also has a suffix rule to search for the corresponding SCCS file, similar to the **.c˜.o** and **.c˜.c** rules shown in this section. The commitment to SCCS support extends even to description files: if you invoke *make* in the absence of a *makefile* or *Makefile*, it looks for *s.makefile* or *s.Makefile*.

A minor feature of *make*, the **.sh** suffix, helps you keep shell scripts under SCCS control. (This feature is not available in all variants; see Appendix C for a way to check your system.) For instance, if you have a script named *chck*, place it under SCCS control as *s.chck.sh*. When you make *chck*, *make* finds the SCCS file (assuming it is newer) and copies it back to *chck*. On some systems, it gives the file executable permission by issuing *chmod*(1).

```
$ make chck
get -p s.chck.sh > chck.sh
cat chck.sh > chck
chmod +x chck
-rm -f chck.sh
```

Adapting make for RCS

Since the popularity of RCS is now about equal to SCCS, many variants of *make* now contain support for both. But even without these variants, you can emulate that support by writing your own suffix rules. The reason you can do it yourself (instead of requiring a special extension, as SCCS did) is that RCS places its special indicator characters **,v** at the end of the filename, not the beginning.

Later in this chapter, we explain how to write your own suffix rules. Even though you can't make complete sense of the following entries without that background, we are including here some sample rules that search for a **.c,v** file—the back-up version of a **.c** file—whenever you try to build a **.c** or **.o** file.

```
CO = co
.c,v.o :
    ${CO} $<
    ${CC} ${CFLAGS} -c $*.c
    - rm -f $*.c
.c,v.c :
    ${CO} $<
```

For extensive RCS support, you have to write rules like these for every type of source file recognized by *make*. If you store files in a different directory, you need to search it through VPATH, as shown earlier for SCCS.

Libraries (Archives)

Libraries—files created with the *ar*(1) utility—tend to be large and internally subdivided. Therefore, *make* offers some special procedures and syntax for maintaining them. Before tackling the *make* rules, let's review the general procedures and terminology regarding libraries.

Imagine that you have created two source files, with several functions in each one:

* *interact.c* containing `intake`, `parse`, and `print`

* *sched.c* containing `cleanup` and `waitloop`

Compilation produces two object files, each containing several modules. Some compilers give each module the exact same name as the C function, while some add a leading underscore. Assuming the latter case, compilation produces:

* *interact.o* containing `_intake`, `_parse`, and `_print`

* *sched.o* containing `_cleanup` and `_waitloop`

You then create a library, which we will call *libops*, from the two object files:

```
ar r libops interact.o sched.o
```

(You might also have to run *ranlib*(1) or some other utility to sort the library, depending on your system and your application.) The resulting structure of *libops* has three levels.

As the diagram shows, *ar* preserves the boundaries between the functions in *interact.o* and *sched.o*. You cannot change an individual function in the library, but you can replace an entire object file. Thus, programmers usually say that *libops* contains the files *interact.o* and *sched.o*. This terminology can be confusing, because *libops* itself is a file, so far as the UNIX file system is concerned. But in the following discussion, we stick to calling *libops* a library, and use the term "file" to refer to any part of the library derived from a particular object file.

Now for using *make*. A simple entry for updating individual object files appeared in Chapter 2, *Macros*. Here it is again:

```
libops : interact.o sched.o gen.o
    ar r $@ $?
```

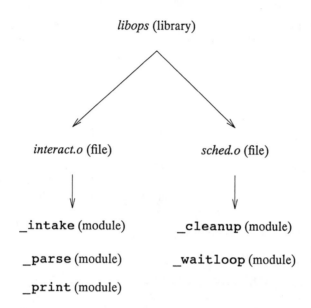

Libraries are commonly listed as prerequisites for executable files, and here they can introduce enormous inefficiency. Take the following example:

```
prog : prog_call.o libops
        ${CC} -o $@ prog_call.o libops
```

Suppose that *sched.c* happens to be newer than *libops*, but your executable file does not need any functions from *sched.c*. Even so, when you build *prog*, you will end up recompiling *sched.c* and replacing *sched.o* in the library.

```
$ make prog
cc -O -c prog_call.c
cc -O -c sched.c
ar r libops sched.o
cc -o prog prog_call.o libops
```

Unless *make* can analyze dependencies on a finer scale, it adds a lot of overhead wherever libraries are undergoing development.

Using Parentheses for Library Modules

To let you specify individual files within the library, *make* extends the syntax of targets and macros to include parentheses. (This feature is not available in all variants; see Appendix C for a way to check your system.) A filename like this:

```
libops(interact.o)
```

or a macro like this:

```
${LIB}(interact.o)
```

is assumed to refer to a library containing an object file. Don't use any spaces within the construct. System V *make* lets you list only one name inside the parentheses, so you have to repeat the entire construct to specify multiple files or modules. Some variants of *make* have removed this restriction.

In some variants of *make*, if you double the parentheses, you can refer to a particular module in the library:

```
libops((_parse))
```

The specific conventions by which the compiler generates module names should be documented for your system. You can also view module names by producing assembly language files with the compiler's –S option, or by running *nm*(1) on an object file, which displays the symbolic names defined in it.

Suffix rules also support the recreation of libraries. Here is the default rule for updating a library when a C source file has changed:

```
.c.a :
        $(CC) -c $(CFLAGS) $<
        ar rv $@ $*.o
        rm -f $*.o
```

Although suffix rules use the conventional suffix **.a** to refer to a library, the actual library name does not have to end with **.a**, as the example below will illustrate. The parentheses are the key that alerts *make* to the presence of a library, and are the only thing necessary to trigger the **.c.a** suffix rule. Also, it is a peculiarity of *make* that *libops(interact.o)* cannot depend on *interact.o*, but only on *interact.c*; that is why the suffix rule refers to **.c** files rather than **.o** files.

A Library Example

What do you gain from all these complicated relationships? In your description file, all you need to do is specify your dependencies on specific files:

```
prog : libops(interact.o) libops(sched.o) prog_call.o
    ${CC} -o $@ prog_call.o libops
```

or even specific modules, if you don't know the files:

```
prog : libops((_parse)) libops((_waitloop)) prog_call.o
    ${CC} -o $@ prog_call.o libops
```

Specifying a module is merely a way to direct *make* to the proper file; there is no way to check whether a particular module changed. For instance, *make* must rebuild the *libops(interact.o)* file when any module in *interact.c* changes, even if you're interested only in *_parse*.

Suppose that *interact.c* has changed since the last time *libops* was built. Either of the entries above causes the commands shown below to execute. The first three commands result from the **.c.a** rule, while the final one comes explicitly from the description file. (The line following the *ar* command is a message that *ar* displays when it replaces *interact.o* in the library.)

```
$ make prog
cc -c -O interact.c
ar rv libops interact.o
r - interact.o
rm -f interact.o
cc -o prog prog_call.o libops
```

While building *libops* in accord with the **.c.a** rule, *make* at first sets its internal macros as follows:

```
$@ = libops
$< = interact.c
$* = interact
```

As each prerequisite is successively treated, $< and $* change accordingly. $@ is not derived from the target, as is normally the case, but rather from the string to the left of the first parenthesis in the current prerequisite—*libops*, in this example. In addition, there is yet one more internal macro we have not previously discussed: $% evaluates to whatever string lies inside the parentheses. In our example:

```
$% = interact.o
```

Of course, you can specify a whole library by name as a target or prerequisite. But specifying files or modules can limit unnecessary builds. If you think it is nit-picking to be so concerned with limiting rebuilds, just enter the following command:

```
ar t /lib/libc.a
```

and count the number of files in this standard library.

Maintaining Libraries

Maintaining libraries is fairly straightforward, so long as the default suffix rules suffice. For instance, you can maintain *libops* with this brief description file entry:

```
libops : libops(interact.o) libops(sched.o)
    echo "$@ is now up-to-date"
```

The special construct referring to library members can also occur as a target in description file entries:

```
libops(interact.o) :  /usr/include/stdio.h
```

In this case, *libops* will be updated if */usr/include/stdio.h* has been changed since the last time time *interact.o* was incorporated into the library.

The command line for making a particular module (that is, updating it in the library) requires that you escape the parentheses to protect them from the shell:

```
$ make libops\(interact.o\)
```

The price of listing files individually is that *make* has to invoke the compiler and *ar* utility separately for each one. Later in this chapter we will see a way to overcome this inefficiency.

The Double Colon

What if you want to use a different set of commands for different files within a single library? Normally, you are not allowed to define the same target twice in your description file, if commands are associated with both instances. But *make* allows you to do this through the use of a double colon.

```
libops :: interact.c
    ${CC} -O -c -DENTRY interact.c
    ar r $@ interact.o
    rm -f interact.o
```

```
libops :: sched.c
    ${CC} -O -c -DRECRD sched.c
    ar r $@ sched.o
    rm -f sched.o
```

make will check both entries whenever it attempts to build *libops*. The commands associated with each prerequisite will execute, if that prerequisite is newer than *libops*.

If you specify a target with double colons, you can't specify it anywhere else in the file with a single colon.

lex and yacc

These utilities are preprocessors that create lexical analyzers and parsers; their output consists of **.c** and **.h** files. If you follow the *make*-established convention of ending *lex* input files with a **.l** suffix and *yacc* input files with a **.y** suffix, *make* handles dependencies neatly. Here is a sample build for a *yacc* input file:

```
$ make program
yacc parse.y
mv y.tab.c parse.c
cc -O -c parse.c
    ...
```

make can check whether its own generated **.c** file is newer than your **.l** or **.y** source, and omit the run of *lex* or *yacc* when possible. Even if you have more than one file to run through *lex* or *yacc*, *make* will not get confused, because the standard *lex.yy.c* and *y.tab.c* files are either removed or renamed to reflect their source.

When you use *lex* and *yacc* together, you must specify the dependencies between their files. The general practice is to run *yacc* with the **-d** option to produce a *y.tab.h* file, and then to refer to this file in the *lex* source through an **#include** statement. Entries like these in your description file ensure accurate rebuilds (assume that the *lex* input file is named *lexer.l* and the *yacc* input file is named *parse.y*):

```
YFLAGS = -d

y.tab.h : parse.y

lexer.o : y.tab.h
```

The Null Suffix

You can define suffix rules using only a single suffix. (This feature is not available in all variants; see Appendix C for a way to check your system.) For example, one of the default suffix rules reads this way:

```
.c :
     $(CC) $(CFLAGS) $(LDFLAGS) $< -o $@
```

In essence, this tells how to make a file with a null suffix (for example, an executable program) from a file with a .c suffix. (Imagine the null suffix inserted between the .c and the colon.) This rule obviates the need for dealing with object files in the case of commands built out of single source files. If the file *program.c* exists in the current directory, and if the single-suffix rule shown above is in effect, then the command,

```
$ make program
```

runs the C compiler on *program.c* to create *program*, as follows:

```
cc -O  program.c -o program
```

Running the C compiler without a −c option results in an automatic invocation of *ld.*

Since the suffix rule illustrated here is in fact one of the default rules, C programs depending on single source files can be made without using any description file at all. If, for example, you have a directory containing source files for the commands, *cat, dd, echo,* and *date* (all built out of single source files), you need only type,

```
$ make cat dd echo date
```

and each of the four source files will be compiled and linked according to the above rule.

How to Display Defaults

At this point, you can get a better handle on *make* if you get to see all its default suffix rules. *make* provides a very useful −p option that prints all the macros, suffix rules, and targets in effect for the current build.

Generating the Display

The following command prints out a couple hundred lines of *make* defaults. The `2>/dev/null` construct will not work in the C shell, but you can just leave it out; all it does is suppress error messages.

```
$ make -fp - < /dev/null 2>/dev/null
```

The **–p** option is the active ingredient here. You probably should redirect the standard output in order to save it in a file.

In order to retrieve a pure list of defaults, unaffected by any description file you might have, the command forces *make* to use null input. The **-f** option and the hyphen standing by itself tell *make* to read the description file from the standard input. But since we use */dev/null* as the standard input, in effect there is no description file.

Error messages (file descriptor *2* in the Bourne shell) have also been redirected to */dev/null*. The messages are very long and contain nothing you are likely to find useful.

Suppose you have changed some defaults in a description file and want to see whether they have taken effect properly. Enter the shorter command,

```
$ make -pns 2>/dev/null
```

which evaluates all the macros and suffix rules in your description file, and then prints out the environment as it is affected by both *make* defaults and your changes. Unfortunately, when you invoke *make* it always tries to make something. If you give it no target, it will try to make the first target in your description file. That is why the command includes **–n** and **–s** options. The first prevents *make* from executing commands, and the second prevents *make* from echoing commands to the standard output.

If you name your description file something other than *makefile* or *Makefile*, specify the name in an **–f** option.

What the Display Means

Now look at the output of the **–p** option. This section goes through each kind of information in the output.

Macro definitions

Usually, macro definitions occur at the head of the listing. The first group of macros consists of your environment variables. If *make* overrides any of them, you can see the new values here. Then come the macros internally defined by *make*:

```
GFLAGS =
GET = get
ASFLAGS =
AS = as
FFLAGS =
FC = f77
CFLAGS = -O
CC = cc
LDFLAGS =
LD = ld
LFLAGS =
LEX = lex
YFLAGS =
YACC = yacc
MAKE = make
$ = $
MAKEFLAGS = b
```

The ones listed above are standard for System V. If your environment includes support for other utilities, you will see them here.

As described earlier, each utility has an accompanying macro for its flags or options. GFLAGS holds *get* options, ASFLAGS holds *as* options, and so on.

The MAKE macro is used for recursive makes, which are described in Chapter 5, *Project Management*. The $=$ definition is the way *make* handles the $$ that begins a shell variable, as explained in Chapter 4, *Commands*. MAKEFLAGS is described in Chapter 6, *Command-line Usage and Special Targets*.

If you invoke *make* recursively—in other words, if your description file issues a *make* or ${MAKE} command—the –p option is not passed down to those makes. This has an impact on the macro definitions you see. People often use *make* recursively to change macro definitions—and these changes would be nice to trace when debugging builds—but the –p option is no help here, because it can report only the top-level definition.

Targets

If you run *make* –p on an actual description file, the macro definitions are followed by the dependency lines and associated commands from your description file. *make* reorders the entries, and expands all the macros on dependency lines.

But the commands themselves are exactly what you put in your files. Here is a sample description file:

```
OBJS = parse.o search_file.o global.o find_token.o

parse: ${OBJS}
    ${CC} ${LDFLAGS} -o $@ ${OBJS}

parse_xdb: ${OBJS}
    ${CC} ${LDFLAGS} -o $@ ${OBJS} /usr/lib/end.o

${OBJS}: parse.h

clean:
    - rm -f *.o core a.out parse parse_xdb
```

and the version printed by the **–p** option:

```
clean:
    - rm -f *.o core a.out parse parse_xdb

parse_xdb: parse.o  search_file.o  global.o  find_token.o
    ${CC} ${LDFLAGS} -o $@ ${OBJS} /usr/lib/end.o

find_token.o: parse.h

global.o: parse.h

search_file.o: parse.h

parse.o: parse.h

parse: parse.o  search_file.o  global.o  find_token.o
    ${CC} ${LDFLAGS} -o $@ ${OBJS}
```

You might also see some rules that *make* defines internally for a target called *markfile*. You can ignore this; it is part of an arcane method for putting version information into executable files for retrieval by the *what*(1) command.

Suffix rules

Finally, the **–p** option shows the suffix rules and the `.SUFFIXES` list. Even if a suffix rule is defined, it takes effect only if both suffixes are in the `.SUFFIXES` list. Wherever your description file redefines a rule, your version of the rule appears instead of the default.

Macros for commands (GET, CC, and so on) as well as their options (GFLAGS, CFLAGS) fit into suffix rules in a very straightforward way. Each rule simply plugs in the proper command and its flags. By default, GFLAGS is undefined, so it is blank. On the other hand, CFLAGS is defined as –O (look back at the macro definitions that came earlier). So you automatically get optimization, unless you pass a different CFLAGS.

Here is a fairly standard set of rules, interspersed with brief comments. The order in which suffix rules are displayed has no significance. The .SUFFIXES list determines their precedence, as we describe later.

The following rule makes it convenient to keep header files under SCCS control:

```
.h~.h:
      $(GET) $(GFLAGS) -p $< > $*.h
```

The following rules build libraries from assembly language, Ratfor, EFL, Fortran, and C files. The suffixes with tildes refer to SCCS files, and therefore start with *get* commands. All the rules clean up after themselves by deleting intermediate files (source or object) after the library is built. The hyphen that you see before some commands means that *make* should continue even if the command fails. This feature is discussed in Chapter 4, *Commands*.

```
.s~.a:
      $(GET) $(GFLAGS) -p $< > $*.s
      $(AS) $(ASFLAGS) -o $*.o $*.s
      ar rv $@ $*.o
      -rm -f $*.[so]

.r~.a:
      $(GET) $(GFLAGS) -p $< > $*.r
      $(FC) -c $(FFLAGS) $*.r
      ar rv $@ $*.o
      rm -f $*.[ro]

.e~.a:
      $(GET) $(GFLAGS) -p $< > $*.e
      $(FC) -c $(FFLAGS) $*.e
      ar rv $@ $*.o
      rm -f $*.[eo]

.f~.a:
      $(GET) $(GFLAGS) -p $< > $*.f
      $(FC) -c $(FFLAGS) $*.f
      ar rv $@ $*.o
      rm -f $*.[fo]

.r.a:
      $(FC) -c $(FFLAGS) $<
      ar rv $@ $*.o
      rm -f $*.o

.e.a:
      $(FC) -c $(FFLAGS) $<
      ar rv $@ $*.o
      rm -f $*.o

.f.a:
      $(FC) -c $(FFLAGS) $<
      ar rv $@ $*.o
      rm -f $*.o
```

```
.c~.a:
     $(GET) $(GFLAGS) -p $< > $*.c
     $(CC) -c $(CFLAGS) $*.c
     ar rv $@ $*.o
     rm -f $*.[co]

.c.a:
     $(CC) -c $(CFLAGS) $<
     ar rv $@ $*.o
     rm -f $*.o
```

The next rules start with *lex* and *yacc* files. There are many such rules, because *make* has to cover every possible dependency. For instance, the source code for a module might be stored as a **.y** file. During a build, *make* might be searching for the prerequisite to a **.c** file or a **.o** file. So it needs both a **.y.c** rule and a **.y.o** rule. This is discussed more in the next section, ".SUFFIXES and Precedence."

```
.l.c:
     $(LEX) $(LFLAGS) $<
     mv lex.yy.c $@

.y~.c:
     $(GET) $(GFLAGS) -p $< > $*.y
     $(YACC) $(YFLAGS) $*.y
     mv y.tab.c $*.c
     -rm -f $*.y

.y.c:
     $(YACC) $(YFLAGS) $<
     mv y.tab.c $@

.l~.o:
     $(GET) $(GFLAGS) -p $< > $*.l
     $(LEX) $(LFLAGS) $*.l
     $(CC) $(CFLAGS) -c lex.yy.c
     rm -f lex.yy.c $*.l
     mv lex.yy.o $*.o

.l.o:
     $(LEX) $(LFLAGS) $<
     $(CC) $(CFLAGS) -c lex.yy.c
     rm lex.yy.c
     mv lex.yy.o $@

.y~.o:
     $(GET) $(GFLAGS) -p $< > $*.y
     $(YACC) $(YFLAGS) $*.y
     $(CC) $(CFLAGS) -c y.tab.c
     rm -f y.tab.c $*.y
     mv y.tab.o $*.o

.y.o:
     $(YACC) $(YFLAGS) $<
     $(CC) $(CFLAGS) -c y.tab.c
     rm y.tab.c
     mv y.tab.o $@
```

Here are all the remaining ways to build object files from various kinds of source code, and their SCCS versions:

```
.s~.o:
    $(GET) $(GFLAGS) -p $< > $*.s
    $(AS) $(ASFLAGS) -o $*.o $*.s
    -rm -f $*.s
.s.o:
    $(AS) $(ASFLAGS) -o $@ $<
.r~.o:
    $(GET) $(GFLAGS) -p $< > $*.r
    $(FC) $(FFLAGS) -c $*.r
    -rm -f $*.r
.e~.e:
    $(GET) $(GFLAGS) -p $< > $*.e
.e~.o:
    $(GET) $(GFLAGS) -p $< > $*.e
    $(FC) $(FFLAGS) -c $*.e
    -rm -f $*.e
.f~.f:
    $(GET) $(GFLAGS) -p $< > $*.f
.f~.o:
    $(GET) $(GFLAGS) -p $< > $*.f
    $(FC) $(FFLAGS) -c $*.f
    -rm -f $*.f
.r.o:
    $(FC) $(FFLAGS) -c $<
.e.o:
    $(FC) $(FFLAGS) -c $<
.f.o:
    $(FC) $(FFLAGS) -c $<
.c~.c:
    $(GET) $(GFLAGS) -p $< > $*.c
.c~.o:
    $(GET) $(GFLAGS) -p $< > $*.c
    $(CC) $(CFLAGS) -c $*.c
    -rm -f $*.c
.c.o:
    $(CC) $(CFLAGS) -c $<
```

As mentioned earlier, **.sh** files are shell scripts:

```
.sh~:
    $(GET) $(GFLAGS) -p $< > $*.sh
    cp $*.sh $*
    -rm -f $*.sh
.sh:
    cp $< $@
```

Here are rules that build an executable file from a single source file:

```
.r~:
    $(GET) $(GFLAGS) -p $< > $*.r
    $(FC) $(FFLAGS) $*.r -o $*
    -rm -f $*.r

.r:
    $(FC) $(FFLAGS) $(LDFLAGS) $< -o $@

.e~:
    $(GET) $(GFLAGS) -p $< > $*.e
    $(FC) $(FFLAGS) $*.e -o $*
    -rm -f $*.e

.e:
    $(FC) $(FFLAGS) $(LDFLAGS) $< -o $@

.f~:
    $(GET) $(GFLAGS) -p $< > $*.f
    $(FC) $(FFLAGS) $*.f -o $*
    -rm -f $*.f

.f:
    $(FC) $(FFLAGS) $(LDFLAGS) $< -o $@

.c~:
    $(GET) $(GFLAGS) -p $< > $*.c
    $(CC) $(CFLAGS) $*.c -o $*
    -rm -f $*.c

.c:
    $(CC) $(CFLAGS) $(LDFLAGS) $< -o $@
```

Finally, the all-important list of suffixes. This forms the subject of the next section.

```
.SUFFIXES: .o .c .c~ .f .f~ .e .e~ .r .r~ .y .y~ .l .l~ \
.s .s~ .sh .sh~ .h .h~
```

.SUFFIXES and Precedence

Previous sections have shown that _make_ can traverse a long chain of dependencies and decide exactly where to start rebuilding. If an object file does not exist, _make_ can find a **.c**, **.f**, or **.s** source file from which to build it. If the source file does not exist, _make_ can go even further and look for an SCCS file. It probably seems a little magical, but when you are trying to debug a description file gone wrong, you had better know how it works.

Let's look at a whole chain of dependencies, and see how *make* succeeds in building an up-to-date object file. Start with a description file containing simply:

```
exec : zapout.o
```

Whether or not *zapout.o* exists, *make* ensures that it is up to date by searching for a source file. Lots of potential rules exist:

```
.c.o:
.c~.o:
.f.o:
.f~.o:
.l.o:
.l~.o:
    .
    .
    .
```

so *make* searches for files according to the order of suffixes in the `.SUFFIXES` list. A standard list like

```
.SUFFIXES: .o .c .c~ .f .f~ .e .e~ .r .r~ .y .y~ .l .l~ \
.s .s~ .sh .sh~ .h .h~
```

tells *make* to look first for a **.c** file, then for a **.c~** file—really the SCCS version of a **.c** file— then a **.f** file, and so on. The default list has been constructed to reflect the number of steps required to process each file. If a **.y** file has already been run through *yacc* to produce a **.c** file, **make** will use that **.c** file and avoid running *yacc* again.

Suppose, however, that you have edited the **.y** file. It will not be forgotten. Before compiling the **.c** file, *make* checks for all of its possible prerequisites. The rules for building **.c** files are:

```
.c~.c:
.l.c:
.y~.c:
.y.c:
```

Following the order in the `.SUFFIXES` list, *make* looks for an SCCS version of the **.c** file, a **.y** file, an SCCS version of the **.y** file, and an **.l** file. So long as the **.c** file is newer than any of these, nothing happens. But if *make* finds that a **.y** file exists that is newer than the **.c** file, it runs *yacc* again.

In short, files that are earlier in the dependency chain should come later in the `.SUFFIXES` list. This minimizes unnecessary rebuilds.

The list also establishes precedence among competing source files. Suppose that—due to an oversight—you have both a Fortran source file named *iod.f* and a C source file named *iod.c*. Every time you make *iod.o*, *make* compiles the **.c** file,

because that comes before **.f** in the list. Even if you put an explicit dependency
line in your description file:

```
iod.o : iod.f
```

make still uses the **.c** file! The dependency line does not override the default suffix rules because there is no command line associated with it. To change this, you
need to put a command in your description file:

```
iod.o : iod.f
        f77 -O iod.f
```

Now *make* uses your command instead of searching for a suffix rule.

Ideally, there should be no need for rules covering more than one step in a chain,
like the **.y.o** rule. If you are building a **.o** file, *make* could theoretically put
together its **.y.c** and its **.c.o** rule and figure out what to do with a **.y** file. And
indeed, some *make* variants have built in this sophistication, as described in
Appendix B, *Popular Extensions*.

But standard *make* is not so clever. It can complete the chain if a **.c** file exists.
But it needs redundant rules like **.y.o** for cases where the **.c** file does not exist. If
you write your own suffix rules, you too must think of every possible relationship
between files in a chain, and write explicit rules for them.

Writing Your Own Suffix Rules

Whenever you find yourself performing a set of commands repetitively over a
variety of files, you can make life easier by generalizing your activities in a
description file. Following the conventions that *make* uses in its default suffix
rules, you can add your own rules and even override the defaults.

Thus, if someone at your site has written a preprocessor that accepts files with a
.prep suffix and generates C source code, you can add **.prep.c** rules to your
description file, integrating the preprocessor into the normal build process. You
can also create rules for activities completely outside the normal scope of *make*,
like the description file shown later in this chapter for producing documents with
troff.

Standard *make* can bind rules only to suffixes, not to other parts of a filename. A
necessary step in generalizing your commands is to choose a suffix that you use
consistently on all files of a given type. Some implementations of *make* have
extended the concept of suffix rules to cover arbitrary character strings, and
sometimes to check other attributes of a file; Appendix B, *Popular Extensions*,
lists a few of these implementations.

To change an existing rule, just include your own rule in the description file. For instance, suppose you always want to move object files to a subdirectory named *objects* after compilation. You could make sure this always happens by defining your own rule for compilation:

```
.c.o :
    $(CC) $(CFLAGS) -c $<
    mv $@ objects
```

When dealing with suffixes not already recognized by *make*, you must create a special target called .SUFFIXES in addition to defining the new suffix rules. For example:

```
.SUFFIXES : .q .w .t

.q.w:
    ...
```

The effect of the .SUFFIXES line is to add .q, .w, and .t to the current list of suffixes. Be sure there are spaces or tabs between the suffixes on this line.

If you define rules for new suffixes without putting them in a .SUFFIXES line, the rules will simply be ignored.

The line

```
.SUFFIXES :
```

deletes all currently recognized suffixes. Therefore, the two lines

```
.SUFFIXES :
.SUFFIXES : .q .w .t
```

replace the current suffixes with .q, .w, and .t. Later we will see why total replacement is sometimes necessary.

You can tell *make* to ignore the default suffixes by invoking it with the **-r** option. Generally, however, this drastic practice would only occur as part of your project's build strategy, and therefore should be enforced within the description file by means of a .SUFFIXES list.

A Sample Collection of Suffix Rules

In this section, we create a description file that prints *troff* documents. This file is not something you can simply plug in where you work, because *troff* utilities and their environment vary too much from one site to the next. Instead, we are using *troff* because it is completely different from building C programs (but still an activity known to most readers) and therefore offers an opportunity to explore the techniques for creating new suffix rules.

Starting assumptions

Formatting with *nroff* or *troff* is an excellent area for automation. A lot of stages and options are visible to the user, but most of the time you want to forget about them and just use one standard process.

First, you pipe your source document through the *pic, eqn,* and *tbl* utilities to process pictures, equations, and tables. Many documents need none of these preprocessors, but it never hurts to run them. Then you run *nroff* for ASCII output or *troff* for laser printer output. In either case, the utility starts by interpreting a package of formatting macros like **–man** or **–ms**, which you specify as a command-line option. (The *troff* macros have nothing to do with *make* macros.) Then *nroff/troff* formats the document. You can store the output in a file, or pipe it to another utility for printing.

The description file that we develop here assumes that all document source files have a **.s** suffix, indicating their use of the **–ms** formatting macros. (You could define similar rules for transforming, say, **.m** files with **-mm** macros and **.e** files with **–me** macros.)

The output of *nroff* or *troff* will be placed in a **.l** file if it was formatted for the line printer, in a **.t** file if formatted for output to a terminal, or in a **.p** file if formatted for a laser printer.

Description file

Here is the complete file for formatting and printing. Refer back to it as you read the next few sections describing it.

The first half of the description file defines a set of general-purpose suffix rules that could be used in numerous description files governing documentation projects. The second half provides the additional information required for one specific project.

```
.SUFFIXES :
.SUFFIXES : .s .t .l .p

PIC = /usr/bin/pic
EQN = /usr/bin/eqn
NEQN = /usr/bin/neqn
TBL = /usr/bin/tbl
NROFF = /usr/bin/nroff ${MACROPACK} ${ROFFARGS} -e
TROFF = /usr/bin/troff ${MACROPACK} ${ROFFARGS}
LP = /usr/bin/lp
UL = /usr/bin/ul
MACROPACK = -ms

.s.l :  # format nroff -ms source file for line printer
    ${NEQN} $< | ${TBL} | ${NROFF} -Tlp -u5 > $*.l
```

```
.s.t :  # format nroff -ms source file for terminal
    ${NEQN} $< | ${TBL} | ${NROFF} -Tlp | ${UL} -i > $*.t

.s.p :  # format troff -ms source file for PostScript laser printer
    ${PIC} $< | ${EQN} | ${TBL} | ${TROFF} -Tpsc > $*.p

#####################################################
# Here begins the specific description file for "book"
#####################################################

FORMATTED = ch01.1 ch02.1 ch03.1 appa.1
CHAPS = ${FORMATTED:.1=}

book : ${FORMATTED}
    ${LP} ${FORMATTED}
    /bin/rm ${FORMATTED}

${CHAPS} : $$@.1
    ${LP} $?
    /bin/rm $?
```

New suffixes

The first line of the description file nullifies the default suffix rules of *make*. The second line establishes four suffixes as significant. These suffixes are interpreted according to the conventions described in the preceding section—because we will base our suffix rules on those same conventions. The reason we did not simply add these suffixes to the existing (default) suffix list is that there are conflicts between the two sets of suffixes. Luckily, a documentation project is not likely to need any of the default suffix rules. But if it did, you could always include the suffixes in your customized .SUFFIXES list.

Suffix rules

In the sample description file, three entries define suffix rules. Note that, while there must be spaces between each suffix in the .SUFFIXES list, there *must not* be a space between the two suffixes on the first line of a suffix rule. Moreover, you must remember that the suffix rule's syntax puts the prerequisite before the target. For example, the first entry declares how to make a .s file into a .l file—that is, it gives the rule for converting a source file containing –ms macros into a formatted output file appropriate for printing on a line printer. Likewise, the third entry shows how to turn a .s file into a .p file, the output for a laser printer.

These rules allow *make* to carry out certain actions even in the absence of any more specific instructions. If your current directory contains a file called *ch01.s*, then these rules alone allow you to type,

```
$ make ch01.1
```

in which case the first suffix rule results in execution of this command:

```
/usr/bin/neqn ch01.s | /usr/bin/tbl | \
    /usr/bin/nroff -ms  -e -Tlp -u5 > ch01.1
```

There are several good reasons for using macros like `${TBL}` and `${EQN}`, instead of specifying the preprocessors literally in the suffix rules. First, they let you use full pathnames while keeping the rules brief. You can also make the description file more modular by nesting macros. For instance, we have decided in this file always to use the **–e** option with *nroff*. It is easier to specify it once in the NROFF macro definition than to remember it every time we write an *nroff* command.

Most important, a thoughtful use of macros allows users to override default definitions where that would be valuable. For instance, if a system offers *lpr* instead of *lp* as the print command, the user could invoke *make* like this:

```
$ make ch01.p LP=lpr
```

More likely, each user would set environment variables in a *.profile* or *.cshrc* startup file, and enforce them by invoking *make -e*. To avoid the need for the **–e** option, some description files leave a macro completely undefined and rely completely on environment variables, as discussed in Chapter 2, *Macros*.

We have used one other technique in anticipation of the user's need to customize a build. The *nroff* and *troff* commands contain a ROFFARGS macro that is not defined in the file. Thus, by default, the macro evaluates to a null string and has no effect. But its presence provides a convenient way for a user to insert extra arguments into the command. By leaving a macro undefined, you are saying to users, "Feel free to add your own options." By defining the macro (even if you define it to be null) you are saying, "This is the right definition; it should be changed only when necessary to adapt to different environments."

The project-specific portion

The rest of the description file is intended to govern a specific writing project—a book consisting of three chapters and one appendix. We have listed the chapters only once, in the FORMATTED macro, so that we only have to update one line in case we add more chapters or appendices later. The CHAPS macro is derived from the FORMATTED macro through string substitution, discussed in Chapter 2, *Macros*.

To keep our description file short, we have shown only how to print the book on a line printer. If no formatted (.l) files currently exist, then making the target **book** results in this execution sequence:

```
$ make book
/usr/bin/neqn ch01.s | /usr/bin/tbl | \
    /usr/bin/nroff -ms  -e -Tlp -u5 > ch01.l
/usr/bin/neqn ch02.s | /usr/bin/tbl | \
    /usr/bin/nroff -ms  -e -Tlp -u5 > ch02.l
/usr/bin/neqn ch03.s | /usr/bin/tbl | \
    /usr/bin/nroff -ms  -e -Tlp -u5 > ch03.l
/usr/bin/neqn appa.s | /usr/bin/tbl | \
    /usr/bin/nroff -ms  -e -Tlp -u5 > appa.l
/usr/bin/lp ch01.l ch02.l ch03.l appa.l
/bin/rm ch01.l ch02.l ch03.l appa.l
```

Since **book** depends on several .l files, and since *make* knows how to create .l files from .s files according to the given suffix rules, this creation takes place automatically. No explicit description file entry is required for making *ch01.l*, *ch02.l*, and so on. Of course, if one or more of the .l files already exist and are up-to-date, they will not be rebuilt.

The final entry in our sample description file was given as

```
${CHAPS} :  $$@.l
    ${LP} $?
    /bin/rm $?
```

which allows you to print one or more individual chapters of the book like this:

```
$ make ch02 ch03
/usr/bin/neqn ch02.s | /usr/bin/tbl | \
    /usr/bin/nroff -ms  -e -Tlp -u5 > ch02.l
/usr/bin/lp ch02.l
/bin/rm ch02.l
/usr/bin/neqn ch03.s | /usr/bin/tbl | \
    /usr/bin/nroff -ms  -e -Tlp -u5 > ch03.l
/usr/bin/lp ch03.l
/bin/rm ch03.l
```

Here `$$@` has evaluated to the current target (*ch02* and *ch03* successively). These targets never exist as files. That is, there is never a file called *ch01* or *ch02*.

As indicated in Chapter 2, *Macros*, the `$?` macro evaluates to the current list of prerequisites that are younger (more recently modified) than the current target. In this case it never refers to more than a single file, since the current target never has more than a single prerequisite. In particular, `$?` always evaluates to some .l file. If a .l file happens to exist, the presence of a .s.l suffix rule tells *make* to compare the last-modified dates of the .s and .l files to determine whether the .l file needs rebuilding.

Shortcuts and variations

Writing description files for documentation projects is challenging, since there are so many possible macro, intermediate file, and output device combinations. We could, for example, have written our first suffix rule this way instead:

```
.s.l :  # format nroff -ms source file & send to printer
        ${NEQN} $< | ${TBL} | ${NROFF} -Tlp -u5 | ${LP}
```

This rule instructs *make* to pipe the formatted file to the print spooler, without ever creating an intermediate file. The **.l** target is called a **dummy target**, because it exists simply as a handle for your suffix rule, rather than as an actual file. You invoke the suffix rule through a command like:

```
$ make ch01.l
```

and then (if the build proceeds without error) go to the printer to pick up your document.

If we want to be able to choose between generating an intermediate file or sending formatted output directly to a printer, we could formulate two rules for each macro / device combination:

```
.s.l :  # format nroff -ms source file for line printer
        ${NEQN} $< | ${TBL} | ${NROFF} -Tlp -u5 > $*.l
.s.lx :  # format nroff -ms source file & send to printer
        ${NEQN} $< | ${TBL} | ${NROFF} -Tlp -u5 | ${LP}
```

This illustrates that a suffix can have more than one letter. (Remember to add the new **.lx** suffix to the `.SUFFIXES` list.) With these rules, we could create a **.l** file from a **.s** file with

```
$ make ch01.l
```

or format and print a **.s** file without leaving any output file to clean up later, by typing

```
$ make ch01.lx
```

Nullifying Rules

Sometimes *make* can derail your description file by finding and invoking a suffix rule that you don't want to use. If you find this happening, you have to trick *make* into running a null command in place of the suffix rule.

The following is adapted from an earlier example of building a library. The goal of the description file is to save time by invoking *cc* and *ar* just once, rather than letting *make* invoke them separately for each file that needs updating.

```
libops :   libops(interact.o) libops(sched.o) libops(objmanip.o)
      $(CC) -c $(CFLAGS) $(?:.o=.c)
      ar rv $@ $?
      rm $?

.c.a :
      true
```

You can depend on *make* to rebuild the out-of-date object files, because it knows enough to check the source file corresponding to each one—for instance, to check whether *interact.c* is newer than *libops(interact.o)*. However, *make* then insists on invoking the **.c.a** rule to rebuild each object file. The whole purpose of this description file is to avoid the **.c.a** rule, but you can do so only by specifying a rule of your own and including a null command.

It is not enough to specify a **.c.a** rule with no commands; you need to give *make* a command to execute—even if it does nothing. The *true*(1) command, a no-op, serves well here. You might even be able to use a semicolon instead of a command, but some versions of the Bourne shell don't accept that.

Another way to override the default rule, just for selected targets, is to list each target with its prerequisite and then specify an empty command. Such explicit dependencies take precedence over any corresponding suffix rules. For example:

```
libops(interact.o) : interact.c
      true
libops(sched.o) : sched.c
      true
libops(objmanip.o) : objmanip.c
      true
```

Using either workaround, the commands come out as shown in the following example when all three library files need updating. The $(?:.o=.c) construct causes **.o** names to become **.c** names through macro string substitution, as described in Chapter 2, *Macros*. *make* executes the null command for each **.c** file. It then executes one command to compile the source files, one to update the archive, and one to remove the object files.

```
true
true
true
cc -c -O interact.c sched.c objmanip.c
ar rv libops interact.o sched.o objmanip.o
rm interact.o sched.o objmanip.o
```

Conflicts With Default Suffixes

When defining your own suffixes and suffix rules, try to avoid using suffixes that already have default meanings for *make*. Since most UNIX systems now support 255-character filenames, there is rarely a reason to restrict yourself to single-character suffixes. However, if you have to re-use a suffix, be sure to rewrite all the existing rules for that suffix—putting in empty commands if necessary.

Here is an example. Suppose you want to add rules to generate C code using your own tool named *regen*, from files that happen to have the suffix **.r**. You may not be aware that this suffix is already meaningful to *make* as marking a source file in Ratfor, an old front-end to Fortran that was popular on UNIX systems many years ago. So even if you create the following, syntactically correct description file, the build will not succeed:

```
.SUFFIXES : .r
.r.c :
    regen $< $@
trac : trac.o
    ${CC} -o $@ trac.o
```

What you want is for *make* to start with *trac.r*, build *trac.c* from it, and then build *trac.o*. But instead *make* uses its own **.r.o** rule, which involves the Fortran compiler.

Once you know that **.r** has a pre-existing meaning, you could change your suffix to something like **.p**, and the description file would work. But what happens if you move to a system that has a Pascal compiler, and the vendor has extended *make* to recognize **.p** as a Pascal file?

The most robust solution is to write a rule going directly from your desired prerequisite to your desired target. The **.r.c** rule is useful for maintaining intermediate **.c** files, but it cannot guarantee the proper generation of **.o** files. What you need most is a **.r.o** rule like the following:

```
.r.o:
    regen $< $*.c
    ${CC} ${CFLAGS} -c $*.c
```

The examples in the last few sections of this chapter have wandered into highly speculative applications. But at some point in your career, you will likely run into subtleties such as these. You cannot always depend on standards remaining unchanged (and the extensions can trip you up the most). We hope that this chapter helps you trace the effects of your customizations and understand how to recover from unexpected impediments.

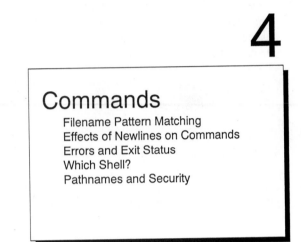

4

Commands

Filename Pattern Matching
Effects of Newlines on Commands
Errors and Exit Status
Which Shell?
Pathnames and Security

Each command executed by *make* behaves as if it were invoked from a shell. Thus, your description file has access to all the familiar and powerful shell features like filename expansion and output redirection:

```
grep '^Error:' ../err[a-z]* | sort >> errorfile
```

But you have to be careful. When you go beyond elementary usage and start to put actual shell scripts in your description file, or when you play with the shell's environment, you need to use special syntax.

Nothing prevents you from entering your commands into a file such as *build_script* and then putting the command

```
sh build_script
```

in your description file. But this might not be any improvement in complexity, if you have to pass a lot of macros to the shell script as variables. Once you understand the issues involved, you can place complicated shell commands right into your description file.

Some people also write shell scripts as wrappers for *make*. That is, instead of running *make* directly, they run a shell script that sets up the environment and executes the *make* command internally. One example appears in Chapter 2, *Macros*.

Broadly speaking, *make* and the shell are just different ways to execute commands. You can use a *make* description file to control everything if the sequence of events is affected mostly by dependencies between files. But it's easier to use a shell script if you have lots of variable manipulation or changes of flow (such as *if* statements or embedded *exit* commands). Each program has its strengths, which is why they are often used together.

Filename Pattern Matching

The shell's filename pattern-matching characters,

```
*  ?  [ ]
```

are expanded in command lines, as well as on the *right* side of the colon in dependency lines. Therefore, the description file entry,

```
print : *.c
    lpr *.c
    date > $@
```

will cause *make* to assume that *print* has a dependency on all files in the current directory with the **.c** suffix, and will print all the **.c** files whenever you make the target, *print*. Incidentally, if the asterisk is at the beginning of a word, *make* includes files that begin with a period, which the shell would not include.

You don't actually see this sort of file substitution often, because *make* offers more reliable ways of specifying multiple prerequisites. Generally, a description file explicitly specifies every prerequisite. *make* can then ignore any temporary scratch files that people add to the directory, and complain if a necessary file disappears.

Effects of Newlines on Commands

make treats each command line as if it were executed in its own shell. Thus, the following sequence—which you probably use every day at your terminal—will not work in *make* as you would expect:

```
cd output
rm *
```

However, the following will work, because both commands are on a single line:

```
cd output; rm *
```

And so will the following, because the backslash combines the commands into a single line conceptually, as far as *make* and the shell are concerned:

```
cd output; \
rm *
```

To understand how you must adapt your shell programming, imagine that you are logging out after each command and logging in again. Anything you did to change the environment is lost. The analogy isn't perfect, because each command starts in the working directory where you issued the *make* command, not in your home directory. Still, the analogy helps to explain a lot of *make*'s special requirements. (For hardened shell users, the true analogy is to say that *make* acts as if you put parentheses around each command line.)

Serious shell programming contains a lot of multi-line constructs such as

```
for i in...done
```

To put these in a description file, use semicolons and backslashes to suppress the shell's interpretation of newlines. For example, consider an entry that compares new and old output from the *spell* utility:

```
1   cat chapter1 chapter2 chapter3 | spell > Newspell
2   if \
3       diff Lastspell Newspell > Spellresult ; \
4   then \
5       rm Newspell Spellresult ; \
6       echo "No changes in spelling" ; \
7   else \
8       mv Newspell Lastspell ; \
9       echo "Changes found in spelling" ; \
10      cat Spellresult ; \
11  fi
```

Lines 2 through 11 comprise a single Bourne shell command. The backslashes suppress the normal interpretation of the newline as a command terminator, resulting in the ten lines being considered as a single line. That is why you need semicolons after each real shell command: without the semicolon, the commands run together and produce syntax errors.

In short, the effect of using backslashes is exactly the same as typing the ten lines (without the backslashes) as a single very long line. *make* passes them to the shell as a valid command:

```
if diff Lastspell Newspell > Spellresult ; then rm Newspell Spellresult ; ...
```

The particular commands in this entry take advantage of a convention whereby *diff* returns a zero status when the files are the same, and a non-zero status when they have any differences. *grep* is another command with similar behavior that you might find useful. Because these commands can return non-zero status codes under perfectly normal (that is, non-error) conditions, you need to protect *make* from terminating after their execution. Ways of handling exit status are discussed later in this chapter.

The description file entry shown above allows you to run your files through *spell* regularly without having to wade through the output, which usually contains a lot of proper names and other words that you want to accept. Before using the entry, you need to run *spell* once on all your source files, ensure that the output is acceptable, and store the output in a file named *Lastspell*. Thereafter, all you have to do is run the *make* entry to keep *Lastspell* up to date. Presumably, you would check the output in *Spellresult* to see whether any of the new words are actually misspelled.

Built-in shell commands, like *cd* and *exit*, have very restricted effects in description files. They only affect the line on which they are located, because *make* starts a new shell for each line. Thus, you cannot use *exit* to cause *make* itself to exit gracefully in the middle of a build. *make* exits only when it is finished with a build, when an individual command produces an error, or when you kill its process.

You can set and use shell variables, but only within a single line. For instance, the following entry concatenates several files into a single *logfile*, and then removes the originals.

```
log :
    for i in tune_file temp_file; do \
        cat $$i >> logfile; \
        rm $$i; \
    done
```

The dollar sign on the shell variable has to be doubled. This is because a single dollar sign in *make* denotes a macro. A double dollar sign in *make* works like a double backslash in the shell: *make* strips off one dollar sign and passes the other to the shell executing the command.

Actual macros in *make* commands are never seen by the shell. It helps here if you understand the order of events: *make* expands all macros during its passes over the description file, before issuing any commands. So you cannot subject macros to traditional shell programming techniques, even though they look like variables upon casual examination. For instance, putting macros in apostophes will not suppress expansion. Complicated expansions like $ {CFLAGS:=-g} will end up as null strings because they have no meaning to *make*.

How do you refer to the shell variable $$, which represents its process number and is often used to generate unique filenames? You can do it, but you just have to double each dollar sign:

```
grep_headers :
    grep '^#[  ]*include' $? > /tmp/gh_$$$$ ; \
    sed 's/^#[  ]*include *//' /tmp/gh_$$$$ \
    .
    .
    .
```

The doubled dollar signs apply to variables only within the shell created by *make*. The doubling is not necessary for the environment variables that you set in your login shell before invoking *make*. As we have seen in Chapter 2, *make* reads your environment and treats these variables as macros.

Shell programming is a daunting subject, with rules of syntax that vary from one construct to another. And yet shell scripts with dozens of lines and multiply-nested constructs have been successfully put into description files. You can do it; but you have to know your shell!

Errors and Exit Status

When a command produces an error—that is, a non-zero exit status—the whole *make* is aborted. Normally, this is a desirable feature. Without it, *make* could turn into the broom of the sorcerer's apprentice, thoughtlessly transferring garbage from one target to the next, and possibly corrupting some irretrievable source files. Still, there are times when you can anticipate and manage errors, and *make* offers some options for continuing when you want it to.

If you put a hyphen before any command, *make* will continue even when that command produces an error. For instance, the following entry tries to put a copy of a new executable file in the */usr/local* directory, which requires root privilege. However, there is no reason to force the whole *make* process to stop just because someone happens to run the entry without root privilege. The hyphen before the *cp* command ensures that the following *rm* command will always execute.

```
plot :
        cc -o $@ basic.c prompt.c
        - cp $@ /usr/local
        rm -f *.o
```

With *mv* and *rm* commands, the –**f** option is quite useful. It lets the commands remove write-protected files without prompting you, and ensures that they return a zero status.

You can force *make* to keep going regardless of command errors by putting the special `.IGNORE` target in your description file, or by invoking *make* with the –**i** option. These features produce the same behavior as putting a hyphen before every command. But they are not recommended, because continuing in the face of unexpected errors can get you into a lot of trouble.

If you are making several independent targets at one time, the –**k** option can be valuable. If *make* encounters an error while making one target, it stops work on that target and on any others that depend on it, but keeps work going on independent targets. Therefore, everything that can correctly be updated will be updated, while other targets remain untouched. *make* tells you which targets were not rebuilt.

For instance, look again at the file from Chapter 1 that made two executable plot programs, *plot_prompt* and *plot_win*. Suppose you entered the command

```
$ make -k plot_prompt plot_win
```

Suppose now that there is a fatal error in the source file that *plot_prompt* depends on, but that the source file is not needed for *plot_win*. Normally, if you try to build both files in a single *make* command, it will stop as soon as it discovers the compilation error. But if you use the –**k** *option, make* will discover its error on *plot_prompt*, leave it untouched, and continue to build *plot_win*.

What if you don't want to ignore errors, but catch them and take some action to recover? Nest the command inside a larger shell construct like an *if* statement.

```
if \
    cp plot /usr/local ; \
then \
    rm -f plot ; \
else \
```

```
        echo 'Cannot move plot to new location' ; \
    fi
```

An error from the *cp* command will not terminate *make* because it is processed by
the surrounding *if* command. If the *cp* is successful, the *rm* command deletes the
old copy of the file; otherwise, the *echo* command prints a message. The exit status of the entire *if* command is returned to *make*, and since both the *rm* and the
echo commands return zero status codes, you are assured that *make* will continue.

You cannot catch errors if you use the **–i** or **–k** options. Since they cause *make* to
keep going in case of error, a zero exit status is always returned. If you want to
use one of the options in an automated procedure, and still be notified when an
error occurs, you have to resort to jerryrigging.

Here is one such workaround, using the kind of wrapper shell script described in
Chapter 2, *Macros*. The script invokes one *make* command to build three programs. Should one build fail, we want *make* to continue, but we also want to be
notified of the failure when the builds are all done. The solution is somewhat
site-specific and crude: make sure the files don't exist when we start, and then
check to see that they're correctly built when we finish. The script also returns an
explicit non-zero exit status in case of error, which was our main goal.

```
rm -f disp trac plot
make -k disp trac plot

stat=0
for executable in disp trac plot
do
  if
    test ! -x $executable
  then
    echo "$executable did not build correctly"
    stat=`expr $stat + 1`
  fi
done

exit $stat
```

We test not only to see whether the file exists, but also whether it is executable.
This is advisable because some linkers, when they fail, leave around a partially
linked file and just don't make it executable. Like all wrapper scripts, this one
makes a lot of assumptions, and will not necessarily do what you want in a different environment.

Which Shell?

Most description files contain commands for the Bourne shell, *sh*. Using the standard Bourne shell maximizes portability, and offers quite adequate programming constructs. (Most people use other shells for their interactive features.)

Some implementations of *make* interpret commands according to the SHELL environment variable. This means that if you normally use the C shell, you can put C shell constructs into your description file, but you will find that the Bourne constructs in preceding sections of this chapter produce syntax errors. Unfortunately, different implementations of *make* are inconsistent. Some insist on using the Bourne shell, under the assumption that most description files are written for it. Some let you specify a different shell through the SHELL macro described in Chapter 2, *Macros*, and some check your environment and use the SHELL variable found there by default. So a description file with complex shell commands can break when moved to a different system, or even when run by a different user.

To write a portable description file, don't depend on the particular behavior of your current *make* or your login shell. Write your commands with just the Bourne shell, and put the following macro definition at the top of every description file to force the use of the Bourne shell:

    SHELL = /bin/sh

If you feel that you absolutely must write some commands under another shell (or under *perl*, *awk*, or some other language) just put them in a separate file and invoke it from the description file. You get the best of both worlds.

Using a non-standard shell for your description file entails subtle risks. Someday, you will share your description file with other people, and they will spend hours trying to figure out why it doesn't work. They might be using a different shell, or using the same shell but defining different aliases.

If you normally log in to the C shell, testing your commands can give you a false sense of security. That is, the commands that work perfectly well at the terminal might not work in a description file. It's possible that you are entering an alias without knowing that it's an alias. Or you might be using the tilde character (˜) for your home directory, forgetting that it has no special meaning in the Bourne shell.

A simple command that requires no shell interpretation—that is, no metacharacters—is executed directly by *make*. Thus, in the following description file entry, *make* consigns the first two commands to the shell, because they contain the >

shell metacharacter. The third command does not require any redirection or other shell processing, so *make* forks and executes it directly.

```
report : datafile1 datafile2 awkfile
    sort -bdf datafile1 datafile2 > /usr/tmp/rptxxx
    awk -f awkfile /usr/tmp/rptxxx > $@
    rm /usr/tmp/rptxxx
```

Bypassing the shell is just a way to save time, and should be invisible to you. But it provides a good reason to avoid aliases, no matter which shell you use in the description file. You might mistakenly use an alias in a command that *make* executes directly. It will then search for an executable file with the name of your alias, and complain when it finds none.

Pathnames and Security

Users' opinions vary about using relative pathnames versus absolute pathnames. A long-standing tenet of UNIX system security has been that automated procedures should carefully control their search paths. In other words, you are advised not to put a simple command like *cat* into a *make* description file—or into a shell script or a crontab entry, for that matter—because you might end up executing a command with the same name from a non-standard directory. To thwart malicious intruders, as well as to prevent honest mistakes, you should specify the full pathname */bin/cat* or set the PATH variable explicitly.

Thus, you will find some description files that use full pathnames for every command. They generally do so by defining a macro for every command that they invoke. The description files end up looking something like this:

```
AWK = /usr/bin/awk
ECHO = /bin/echo
SORT = /bin/sort

defs :
    ${ECHO} "Listing header files"
    ${AWK} -f awkscript *.h | ${SORT} > $@
    .
    .
    .
```

The user can still override each macro on the command line, if necessary.

New system configurations and build procedures are undermining the policy of hard-coded paths. With systems coming on and off networks, directories being mounted and unmounted, and build environments splitting along multiple dimensions, search paths can easily change each week. Many development teams cannot afford to hard-code their paths any more than they can hard-code constants in their C code. So they are deliberately using environment variables to specify the names of directories, as well as the search paths used in shell scripts and description files. Security is sought through other means. The description files tend to look like this:

```
SRC_DIR = ${PROJECT_TREE}/src
defs : ${INCL}/errno.h
    cd ${SRC_DIR} ; ...
```

Each user is supposed to set **PROJECT_TREE** and **INCL** as environment variables in a login file. To work on a different aspect of a project, they might redefine these variables, thereby running the same description files with completely different effects.

The pressures placed on *make* by large projects and by the evolution of UNIX systems come in many guises. These are explored in the next chapter.

5

Project Management

Dummy Targets
Recursive make on Directories
General Tips on Recursive make
Other Techniques for Multiple Directories
Compiler Options and #ifdef directives
Header Files
Global Definitions (include Statement)
Distributed Files and NFS Issues

When projects grow (as most do) to involve teams of programmers on many systems and multiple variants of software in simultaneous use, *make* takes on a very different appearance. The description files must be longer and more complex, because one cannot rely as much on default rules. Some sophisticated techniques, like recursion, become regular necessities.

One of the best things one can say about *make*, as with UNIX systems in general, is that it is powerful enough to overcome its own limitations. But large projects strain *make* seriously. Some of the classic areas of difficulty include:

• Builds covering more than one directory. It takes some work to get *make* to check for dependencies and apply suffix rules across directories.

• Variation in compiler options, which can become quite complex when you use conditional preprocessor directives like **#if**. *make*'s simple check for the last-modified time of a file cannot take such variations into account.

• Hidden dependencies, notably involving **.h** header files. You must tell *make* explicitly about each such dependency.

To be fair to *make*, many of the problems for which it is blamed actually stem from restrictions imposed by the compilers or other elements of UNIX systems. Some may even be inseparable from the organizational problems of large software projects. For instance, when several people have different versions of a file in their personal directories, keeping track of versions requires good planning and organization, and cannot be solved simply with automated tools.

Yet everyone agrees that *make* has too many limitations. One reason that it appears so powerful is that it relies on some unstated assumptions, as well as the restrictions enforced by the programming utilities on UNIX systems. The clever way in which *make* searches for prerequisites and applies suffix rules, for instance, rests on the compiler's strict file-naming conventions.

Over the decades, programmers have learned how to get the most out of *make* in these demanding circumstances. A sort of subculture has grown up with recognized conventions and practices. A number of people go even further and formalize the workarounds into tools layered on top of *make* or even attempt to supersede it. Appendix B, *Popular Extensions*, lists some of the public domain tools. Finally, many implementations of *make* contain minor extensions to ease the difficulties, and once you understand the issues you can check your site's documentation to find out what your implementation offers.

Dummy Targets

Throughout this book you have seen examples of targets that are not actual files, but simply convenient names for common activities. Often, such targets represent combinations of builds:

```
all : disp trac plot

disp :
    ${CC} -o $@ src/interact_objs -lX11

trac :
    .
    .
    .
```

When programmers distribute such a description file with a software package, they can tell casual users simply to enter

```
$ make all
```

and the users ideally end up with a complete, working environment, without needing to understand the various parts of the package. In fact, description files enclosed with released software generally have a target called *install*, which covers both building the executable files and moving them to their final locations. Another common target, *clobber*, tries to undo the installation by removing any files built by earlier *make* runs.

```
INSTALLDIR = /usr/local

install : disp trac plot
    cp -f disp ${INSTALLDIR}
    cp -f trac ${INSTALLDIR}
    cp -f plot ${INSTALLDIR}
    cd ${INSTALLDIR}; \
    chmod 755 disp trac plot; \
    chgrp bin disp trac plot; \
    chown bin disp trac plot

clobber :
    rm -f *.o disp trac plot
    cd ${INSTALLDIR}; \
    rm disp trac plot
```

Since *install* lists the executable files as prerequisites, *make* builds them first. If the builds are successful, it proceeds to the commands listed under *install*.

Essentially, dummy targets—and dummy prerequisites—let you step outside the normal chain of dependencies between files, and force something to happen. Many applications of the technique appear in this chapter. While *make* checks timestamps on real files, it uses somewhat arbitrary rules for dependencies involving dummy targets and prerequisites:

- A dummy target (a non-existent file that appears before the colon on a dependency line) is always out of date, and therefore always causes its associated commands to execute.

- A dummy prerequisite (a non-existent file that appears after the colon on a dependency line) is always more up to date than its target, and therefore always causes its target to be rebuilt.

If you use a non-existent filename as a prerequisite, it must appear somewhere else as a target, even if no commands appear after it; otherwise *make* will stop with a complaint that it doesn't know how to make the file.

A subtle variation on these dummy targets is the target that actually represents a file, but one whose existence merely records the completion of an activity. For instance, the following entry strips unneeded symbol information from executable files:

```
stripsync : disp trac plot
    strip $?
    touch $@
```

The *disp*, *trac*, and *plot* prerequisites are executable programs. The $? macro contains the prerequisites that are newer than *stripsync*. The final *touch* command creates *stripsync*, or changes its last-modified timestamp if the file already exists. But because nothing else uses *stripsync*, it is empty. Why then does the description file create it? The timestamp on the file lets *make* know whether or not the prerequisites have been stripped. You can "build" the target any time, and if no out-of-date files exist, *make* will simply report:

```
$ make stripsync
`stripsync´ is up to date.
```

and not bother to run the *strip* command. Such a target—which is really a form of communication between successive *make* invocations—illustrates a general practice that is fairly common on UNIX systems: using files to synchronize unrelated processes.

This kind of target is fragile because an unknowing user might see the empty file and delete it, not realizing its purpose. A better practice would be to store something like the following in the file, just for documentation purposes:

```
stripsync : disp trac plot
    strip $?
    echo "Last time executables were stripped:\c" > $@
    date >> $@
```

Recursive make on Directories

make is happiest when you keep all your files in a single directory. But on large projects, this is not feasible. Typically, your builds will combine a number of files from directories shared by many project members, and perhaps some personal files of your own.

Most projects accommodate *make* by structuring their source files into a strict hierarchical set of directories, which is a useful technique for maintenance in any case. Here is a simple example, where a *disp* directory contains two subdirectories of source files named *fig* and *structops*:

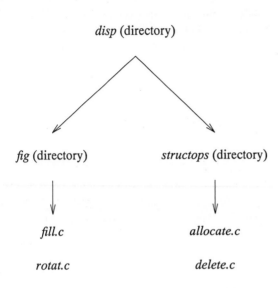

disp (directory)

fig (directory)   *structops* (directory)

fill.c   *allocate.c*

rotat.c   *delete.c*

The cleanest way to build is to put a separate description file in each subdirectory, and tie them together through a master description file that invokes *make* recursively. While cumbersome, the technique is easier to maintain than a single, enormous description file that covers multiple directories.

For our simple program, *disp/fig/makefile* consists of just one line:

```
all : fill.o rotat.o
```

while *disp/structops/makefile* contains:

```
all : allocate.o delete.o
```

Finally, the top-level *disp/makefile* ties everything together. The *fig_obj* and *structops_obj* targets are dummy targets—no files with those names exist:

```
OBJS =    fig/fill.o \
          fig/rotat.o \
          structops/allocate.o \
          structops/delete.o

disp : fig_obj structops_obj
      ${CC} ${LDFLAGS} -o $@ ${OBJS}

fig_obj :
      cd fig ; make all

structops_obj :
      cd structops ; make all
```

If recursive *make* confuses you, look at the following commands that are executed when you enter the *make* command in the top-level *disp* directory. Basically, you execute the description file in the *fig* directory, then the description file in the *structops* directory, and finally the *cc* command under the target *disp*:

```
$ make
cd fig ; make all
cc -O -c fill.c
cc -O -c rotat.c
cd structops ; make all
cc -O -c allocate.c
cc -O -c delete.c
cc -o disp fig/fill.o fig/rotat.o structops/allocate.o structops/delete.o
```

By keeping each object file in the same directory as its source file, you can take advantage of the usual *make* suffix rules and modification checks. If you decide to keep source files and object files in separate directories, you have to throw out default rules and specify every dependency manually. Other sections of this chapter show how to keep source files in a common area used by all project members, while storing object files in the directories where you build executable files.

If recursive *make* still seems confusing or unnecessarily complicated, you have more chances to see it in action later in this chapter.

General Tips on Recursive make

The previous section showed a frequently-encountered situation where it is valuable to invoke *make* within your description file. Later sections of this chapter touch on some other common uses for recursive makes: to pass different compiler options for different files, and to force rebuilds of up-to-date files.

In general, recursive *make* solves problems where you want to determine information dynamically during your build, and pass that information on to other parts of the build. For instance, suppose several of your entries have to know the type of a particular file. You can store this information in the macro FTYPE, and then proceed to build your targets with that macro defined:

```
all :
    make conv sys "FTYPE=`file a.out | sed 's/.*: *//'`"
sys :
    @ echo Building $@ with file type ${FTYPE}
    . . .

conv :
    @ echo Building $@ with file type ${FTYPE}
    . . .
```

The actual commands used to extract the file type are simplified for this example. When you make the dummy target *all*, the results are:

```
$ make all
make conv sys "FTYPE=`file a.out | sed ´s/.*: *//´`"
Building conv with file type pure executable not stripped
Building sys with file type pure executable not stripped
```

Although the description files so far have referred to the *make* command directly, it is actually better to use the internal MAKE macro. (This feature is not available in all variants; see Appendix C for a way to check your system.)

```
fig_obj :
    cd fig ; ${MAKE} all
```

The advantage is that MAKE passes along the options that you enter on your original command line. For instance, if you enter *make −n* to look at your commands without executing them, the **−n** option applies to recursive *make* as well. In fact, **−n** is quite useful if you want to see which targets need updating in a tree of recursively-invoked description files. Chapter 6, *Command-line Usage and Special Targets*, explains the option in more detail.

Some options are not passed when you invoke **${MAKE}**. One is **−f**; when you use a non-standard name for your description file, you must always specify it in the command. For instance, if you want to build the target *all* listed in the file *test.mk*, you have to use the following command, even within the *test.mk* file itself:

```
${MAKE} −f test.mk all
```

The other options suppressed by recursive makes are **−d** and **−p**, which are generally for debugging.

Each invocation of *make* starts off with a fresh set of macro definitions. In other words, *make* does not automatically pass down the macro definitions that you set at the top level. Thus, each *make* command in a description file should specify any macros that might be important—such as CFLAGS, names for directories, and so forth. A typical recursive *make* command looks like this:

```
all :
    ${MAKE} disp trac plot "CFLAGS=${CFLAGS}" \
        "LDFLAGS=${LDFLAGS}" "INCLUDES=${INCLUDES}" "FRC=${FRC}"
```

where each of the complicated arguments in double quotes is simply passing down your top-level definition for CFLAGS, LDFLAGS, and so on. Note that, as explained in Chapter 2, *Macros*, these command-line definitions take precedence over both shell environment variables and macro definitions contained in the description files.

If you want to add some option to CFLAGS—such as a **–D** option to define a symbol—without modifying the existing definition of `CFLAGS`, use this command line:

```
${MAKE} disp trac plot "CFLAGS=${CFLAGS} -DBSD" ...
```

Remembering to pass down the significant variables from one *make* to another can be difficult. Some people make things easier on themselves by eliminating the command arguments and setting environment variables instead. So long as the description file does not define a macro, you can set an environment variable to the desired value and it will be passed to every invocation of *make*. See Chapter 2, *Macros*, for a discussion of using environment variables to set defaults.

But when you make a procedure easier, you often makes errors easier, too. If you don't explicitly set things in a description file, and a build goes wrong, then you may have trouble figuring out which macros are significant and where their values are defined.

Other Techniques for Multiple Directories

If you have to pull just a few files from a directory located elsewhere on the system, it might be appropriate to use the brute force approach and specify each full pathname. But *make* offers a few tricks for handling directories.

Directories in Internal Macros

(This feature is not available in all variants; see Appendix C for a way to check your system.) All internal macros except **$?** can take a D or F modifier. These have the effect of truncating file pathnames referred to by the macros; D truncates the pathname so that only the directory portion of the name remains, while **F** truncates to the file portion of the name. If, for example, **$<** currently represents:

```
/usr/jobstor/work/math.c
```

then $ { <D} evaluates to:

```
/usr/jobstor/work
```

and `${<F}` evaluates to:

```
math.c
```

You might therefore have the following description file entry:

```
modules : /usr/jobstor/sys/io.o /usr/jobstor/work/math.o
    cd ${<D}; make ${<F}
```

Each directory of source files, */usr/jobstor/sys* and */usr/jobstor/work*, should contain its own description file. The entry shown above invokes *make* recursively, building *io.o* in */usr/jobstor/sys* and *math.o* in */usr/jobstor/work*.

Here is a complete list of F-modified macros:

${@F}   File portion of current target.

$${@F}   File portion of current target (as a prerequisite in dependency lines).

${<F}   File portion of current prerequisite.

${*F}   File portion of current prerequisite without suffix.

${%F}   File portion of .o file corresponding to current target (valid but not too useful).

All of the corresponding D-modified macros are also valid.

Used with a simple (relative) filename, the D modifier evaluates to a period (.), which means the current directory. So you can always employ such a macro safely—in *cd* commands, for instance.

Viewpath (VPATH Macro)

Some implementations of *make* let you specify a list of directories to search for the files it needs, in the form of a macro called VPATH. The list of directories is called the viewpath, and it works like the PATH variable in the shell.

If your implementation of *make* supports viewpaths, you can use a description file like this:

```
VPATH = /usr/src
OBJS = main.o allocate.o delete.o

structops : ${OBJS}
    ${CC} -o $@ ${OBJS}

main.o : main.c
```

```
allocate.o : allocate.c

delete.o : delete.c
```

make now goes to two places when searching for each prerequisite: first your current directory, then */usr/src*. For instance, if your current directory does not have an *allocate.c* file, *make* looks for */usr/src/allocate.c* .

It is an unfortunate weakness of some *make* variants that they use VPATH to search only for prerequisites that you explicitly list in dependency lines. In these variants, VPATH will not help *make* find the **.c** file that a **.o** file implicitly depends on. That is why the preceding example included an extra dependency line for each object file. Try VPATH on your system, both with and without the explicit dependency lines. You might find that you don't need them.

VPATH can specify multiple directories separated by colons. For example, the definitions,

```
VPATH = mysrc:${DIRS}
DIRS = /usr/src:/release/src
```

tell *make* to search the following directories, in order, before giving up:

- the current directory (this is always first)

- *mysrc* (a subdirectory of where you are now)

- */usr/src*

- */release/src*

Thus, you can work on your own temporary copies of source files, storing them in the same directory as your *make* description file, and be assured that *make* uses them whenever they match a component. But you can also send *make* on a search through the project's common set of files, when you don't have a copy of your own.

When VPATH is set by the user instead of the description file, it becomes a versatile tool for handling variants. Suppose that object files for your project reside in two directories:

/usr/src   A complete set of source files that build a stable version.

mysrc   Your personal versions of some source files.

If you create a description file in a common area with no VPATH definition in it, everyone can build the proper version of *structops* using the same file. When you build your personal version, you enter

```
$ make -f /usr/src/Makefile structops "CFLAGS=-g -DDEBUG" \
    VPATH=mysrc:/usr/src
```

where the VPATH tells *make*, in effect, "Look first in the current directory, then in *mysrc*, and finally in the project's directory of stable source files."

Meanwhile, another member of the team can build a stable version of the program by entering

```
$ make -f /usr/src/Makefile structops CFLAGS=-O VPATH=/usr/src
```

Besides source files, VPATH can be useful for finding libraries that the linker needs to search.

VPATH has been in *make* for a long time, so most versions support it. But for some reason it often goes undocumented. Try it out, even if your system's documentation doesn't mention it. (A simple shell script testing VPATH is in Appendix C, *Features That Differ Between Variants of* make.)

The implications of search paths are often more complicated than they may seem. VPATH certainly has its share of quirks. It's worth spelling out here the pitfalls you are most likely to encounter.

First, different variants demonstrate infuriating differences in when they use VPATH. Some use it when searching for prerequisites but not for targets; others use it for targets but not prerequisites.

Some variants are overly eager to use the viewpath. BSD 4.3 *make* searches it for every word on every command line. In fact, some versions of *make* will use VPATH in searching for anything imaginable—including the files specified in `include` statements, and even the description file itself! Actual errors have also been found, where the executable program—the target in the *make* command—has been left somewhere on the viewpath, instead of the current directory.

To avoid possible confusion, we recommend that you use VPATH just for the first stage in the chain of dependencies: finding source files. Each person building an executable file should keep object files in the current directory where the *make* is taking place. Since the compiler leaves its output in the current directory, this rule is not hard to follow.

Here is another problem with VPATH: prerequisites with relative pathnames are handled inconsistently by different implementations of *make*. Some use VPATH to search for the prerequisites and some don't. If you have a description file with

```
VPATH = /usr/include

prog : sys/types.h
```

some versions of *make* (those that are based on System V) will find */usr/include/sys/types.h* . But BSD *make* looks for a subdirectory named *sys* in your current directory, and then gives up with the complaint,

```
Don't know how to make types.h.
```

It's best not to expect searches for subdirectories anyway. If you want to search */usr/include/sys* , just include it in VPATH.

The D and F modifiers introduced in the previous section don't mix well with VPATH. If you assume that the F modifier always returns a simple filename—usually a dependable feature—and you define VPATH, you will be in trouble.

To sum up, VPATH is very useful in particular circumstances that fit what it has to offer. In these circumstances, it is a welcome replacement for the technique of placing a description file in every directory and using recursive *make*. But VPATH is by no means a comprehensive solution to the problem of multiple directories, and it is not completely portable. For a summary of implementation-dependent features in VPATH, see Appendix C.

Compiler Options and #ifdef directives

Conditional compilation, through preprocessor directives like **#ifdef** and **#ifndef**, is unavoidable in a world of evolving software. Some of the alternatives reflect the need to compile and run on different hardware or operating systems:

```
#ifdef BSD
    struct timeval timeout={1,0};
#endif
    . . .
sp_mask = 1<<sp_fd;
#ifdef BSD
    if ( select(sp_fd+1, &sp_mask, &sp_mask, &sp_mask, timeout) > 0)
#else
    if ( select(sp_fd+1, &sp_mask, &sp_mask, &sp_mask, 1000) > 0)
#endif
    . . .
```

while some constructs just contain temporary, personal experiments and debugging aids:

```
#ifdef STATS
    long cnt=0;
#endif

#ifdef STATS
    ++cnt;
#endif
```

To compile the statements you want, define the proper symbols in CFLAGS. For instance, the following *make* command compiles all source files with the BSD and STATS symbols defined:

```
$ make -f trac.mk trac "CFLAGS = -DBSD -DSTATS"
```

If the command line gets so long that it is hard to type, or if you want to pass different symbols to various object files, recursive *make* comes in handy. Given the following entry:

```
full_test :
    make trac.o "CFLAGS = -DSTATS -DBSD"
    make main.o "CFLAGS = -DBSD"
    ${CC} -o $@ trac.o main.o
```

all you have to do is make *full_test*, and *make* passes the right **–D** option to each command as follows:

```
$ make full_test
make trac.o "CFLAGS = -DSTATS -DBSD"
cc -DSTATS -DBSD -c  trac.c
make main.o "CFLAGS = -DBSD"
cc -DBSD -c  main.c
cc -o full_test trac.o main.o
```

Many variants of *make* support conditional macro definitions. This small enhancement is so useful for manipulating compiler options that we must mention it, even though it is not part of the standard System V *make.* The syntax typically looks like this:

```
trac := CFLAGS = -DBSD
full_test := CFLAGS = -DSTATS -DBSD
```

The effect is to define **CFLAGS** as **–DBSD** whenever the target is *trac*, and as **–DSTATS –DBSD** whenever the target is *full_test*.

One big problem with conditional compilation—and any other variation in compiler options—is that you cannot tell, just by looking at the names of the object files, which symbols were used in compiling each one. Neither can *make*. To illustrate the problem, suppose your directory contains the following files before you begin your build:

```
makefile main.c trac.c trac.o
```

and *trac.o* is newer than *trac.c*. *make* will use the existing *trac.o* instead of recompiling. This could be disastrous. For all you know, *trac.o* might have been compiled without **−DSTATS**, and you could end up with a severely corrupted executable file.

No perfectly satisfactory solution exists in standard *make*. Programmers generally fall back on two kinds of workarounds: forcing remakes of up-to-date files, and preserving different variants of files under different names or directories.

Forcing Remakes

A brute-force method of ensuring consistent object files is to delete all of the existing object files before rebuilding:

```
full_test : clean        # always makes clean first
    make trac.o "CFLAGS = −DSTATS −DBSD"

clean :                  # removes executable and objects
    − rm −f full_test *.o
```

More commonly, programmers trick *make* into rebuilding selected targets by adding extra dependencies. Here is the classic method (used in many System V description files):

```
rebuild :
    make thk.o FRC=force_rebuild

force_rebuild :

thk.o : ${FRC}
```

You need to define a macro such as **FRC**, and a dummy target such as *force_rebuild*. The traditional description files use the name **FRC** for both the macro and the dummy target, but this is unnecessary and makes the trick very hard to understand. We have arbitrarily chosen a different name for the dummy target here.

At the heart of the trick is *make*'s interpretation of file dependencies. By definition, a non-existent prerequisite is always more up to date than its target. So if the real file *thk.o* depends on the non-existent file *force_rebuild*, *make* will recompile *thk.o*.

But you presumably want a choice whether or not to rebuild *thk.o*. This is where the FRC macro comes in. Normally it is null, so *thk.o* doesn't depend on anything except *thk.c*. If you want to force *make* to recompile, enter:

```
$ make rebuild
```

This command sets the FRC macro, and suddenly *thk.o* depends on a dummy target. Therefore, *make* rebuilds *thk.o*. This is the kind of feature that you might have to play with to understand. And when you do, you will understand description files like this, where you choose the value for FRC, and the *all* target merely passes it on while making multiple targets:

```
ENTER_OBJS = parse.o find_token.o global.o
TESTEX_OBJS = parse.o find_token.o global.o interact.o
LIBRARIES = -lm

all :
        make enter testex "CFLAGS=${CFLAGS}" "FRC=${FRC}"

enter : ${FRC}
        make ${ENTER_OBJS} "CFLAGS=${CFLAGS}" "FRC=${FRC}"
        ${CC} -o $@ ${ENTER_OBJS} ${LIBRARIES}

testex : ${FRC}
        make ${TESTEX_OBJS} "CFLAGS=${CFLAGS}" "FRC=${FRC}"
        ${CC} -o $@ ${TESTEX_OBJS} ${LIBRARIES}

parse.o find_token.o interact.o : parse_defs.h ${FRC}

global.o : parse_defs.h extra_defs.h ${FRC}

force_rebuild :
```

If you just want to update some targets from existing files, issue the command

```
$ make all
```

To start a complete rebuild that recompiles all objects, issue the command

```
$ make all FRC=force_rebuild
```

Let's look at the output of the second command, to see what effect the FRC macro has:

```
make enter testex "CFLAGS=-O" "FRC=force_rebuild"
make parse.o find_token.o global.o "CFLAGS=-O" "FRC=force_rebuild"
cc -O -c parse.c
cc -O -c find_token.c
cc -O -c global.c
cc -o enter parse.o find_token.o global.o -lm
make parse.o find_token.o \
    global.o interact.o "CFLAGS=-O" "FRC=force_rebuild"
cc -O -c parse.c
cc -O -c find_token.c
```

```
cc -O -c global.c
cc -O -c interact.c
cc -o testex parse.o find_token.o global.o interact.o -lm
```

First, the *all* target invokes a recursive make on *enter*. Because FRC is defined as *force_rebuild*, the *enter* target depends on *force_rebuild*. And therefore *enter* must be remade.

Check now the dependency lines for the object files. Each of them depends on ${FRC}, and therefore on *force_rebuild*. So they too must be remade.

After *enter* is remade, the turn comes for *testex*. Here again, the object files are recompiled. The recompilation happens to be inefficient because CFLAGS is the same, but in forcing rebuilds we are more interested in being comprehensive than in being efficient.

To sum up, the ${FRC} macro travels back along the chain of dependencies, so long as you:

1. Use recursive makes with the argument "FRC=${FRC}".

2. Specify that every file depends on ${FRC}.

In the preceding example, you might have noticed, the dependency lines for the targets *enter* and *testex* do not specify any prerequisites. In most description files, the dependency lines routinely list all the objects that an executable file requires. But that would be redundant when you are invoking *make* recursively. If you specified the objects both on the dependency line and in the *make* command, you would get:

```
cc -O -c parse.c
cc -O -c find_token.c
cc -O -c global.c
make parse.o find_token.o global.o "CFLAGS=-O" "FRC=force_rebuild"
cc -O -c parse.c
cc -O -c find_token.c
cc -O -c global.c
```

In other words, any out-of-date object files would be built twice.

Some variants of *make* preserve the most recent state of each target—that is, the CFLAGS and other macros used to build the target—in a special state file. Therefore, if you make a target once with "CFLAGS=-DBSD" and again with "CFLAGS=-DSTATS -DBSD", the state file lets *make* know that it must recompile the object files. So long as you use the same description file and do nothing else to confuse *make*, this enhancement is a valuable alternative to forced rebuilds.

Maintaining Multiple Variants Through Explicit Targets

A more difficult but efficient way to manage files, in an environment where compiler options can vary, is to maintain multiple copies of object files under different names. In the following example, building *trac* causes the source files to be compiled using the default rules, while building *full_test* causes the same source files to be compiled with special options, and renames the resulting object files. Because you always preserve the different versions under different names, you can always use an existing **.o** file with the assurance that it was compiled the way you want. (Alternatively, you could build the object files in *full_test* with recursive *make* commands, as shown earlier, and then rename them.)

```
OBJS = trac.o main.o
OBJS_STATS = trac_stats.o main_stats.o

trac : ${OBJS}
    ${CC} -o $@ ${OBJS}

full_test : ${OBJS_STATS}
    ${CC} -o $@ ${OBJS_STATS}

trac_stats.o : trac.c
    ${CC} ${CFLAGS} -DSTATS -DBSD -c $?
    mv trac.o $@

main_stats.o : main.c
    ${CC} ${CFLAGS} -DSTATS -DBSD -c $?
    mv main.o $@
```

Some compilers let you specify object filenames during compilation. Others force you to use the same name every time you compile, so you must explicitly rename the object file, as shown above.

Maintaining Multiple Variants in Different Directories

A variant of the last solution is to set up separate directories for separate versions, and to build each version in the appropriate directory. This is a natural solution for large project teams, where different versions are likely to be stored in different people's directories anyway.

The example from the previous section could be handled through three directories. Suppose, for the sake of simplicity, that all are subdirectories under one top-level directory. One subdirectory is named *src*, and contains the source files *main.c* and *trac.c*. The second is named *trac*, and starts out containing just the following *makefile*:

```
OBJS = trac.o main.o
CFLAGS = -DBSD

trac : ${OBJS}
     ${CC} -o $@ ${OBJS}

trac.o : ../src/trac.c
     ${CC} ${CFLAGS} -c $?

main.o : ../src/main.c
     ${CC} ${CFLAGS} -c $?
```

The third is named *full_test*, and contains the following *makefile*. The only significant change is the addition of **-DSTATS** to the definition of **CFLAGS**.

```
OBJS = trac.o main.o
CFLAGS = -DBSD -DSTATS

full_test : ${OBJS}
     ${CC} -o $@ ${OBJS}

trac.o : ../src/trac.c
     ${CC} ${CFLAGS} -c $?

main.o : ../src/main.c
     ${CC} ${CFLAGS} -c $?
```

(If your variant of *make* supports VPATH, the description files could be even simpler. All of the entries that build object files could be omitted, because suffix rules would handle them properly.)

A sample build of *full_test* yields:

```
$ cd full_test
$ make
cc -DBSD -DSTATS -c ../src/trac.c
cc -DBSD -DSTATS -c ../src/main.c
cc -o full_test trac.o main.o
```

Each directory contains object files built with the appropriate compiler options. If a source file changes, *make* performs its usual dependency analysis and rebuilds the object file.

To tie the versions together in one description file in the top-level directory, you could use the following description file:

```
final_build :
     cd trac ; make trac

test_build :
     cd full_test ; make full_test
```

Maintaining Variants Through Suffix Rules

This elegant solution uses the best features of *make*. As in the previous sections, object files are distinguished by their names, but in this case the suffix is the distinguishing feature. For profiling, many people use a **.p** suffix. The same old example we've been looking at now uses the following description file:

```
OBJS = trac.o main.o
OBJS_STATS = trac.p main.p
CFLAGS = -DBSD

.SUFFIXES : .p

.c.p :
        ${CC} ${CFLAGS} -DSTATS -p -c $<
        mv $*.o $@

trac : ${OBJS}
        ${CC} -o $@ ${OBJS}

full_test : ${OBJS_STATS}
        ${CC} -o $@ -p ${OBJS_STATS}
```

Thus, the profiled version, *full_test*, depends on *trac.p* and *main.p*. Don't be confused by the **.p** suffixes. These files are simply object files under a different name, as the **.c.p** rule shows. Most compilers are strict about naming conventions when creating object files, but when it comes to the executable file, anything goes. A sample build of *full_test* produces

```
$ make full_test
cc -DBSD -DSTATS -p -c trac.c
mv trac.o trac.p
cc -DBSD -DSTATS -p -c main.c
mv main.o main.p
cc -o full_test -p trac.p main.p
```

Header Files

make cannot look inside files to see hidden dependencies. So it does not know which **#include** directives are within each file, and cannot automatically rebuild an object file if the header file changes. Most description files therefore specify the dependencies directly:

```
OBJS = parse.o search_file.o global.o find_token.o

{OBJS} : parse_defs.h

global.o : extra_defs.h
        . . .
```

The programmer added these dependencies because all the source files include *parse_defs.h*, and *global.c* includes *extra_defs.h* as well. Thus, if a *global.o* exists, *make* does not assume it is up-to-date until its last modification time is checked against *parse_defs.h*, *extra_defs.h*, and (because of the suffix rules) *global.c*. A change to any of these files forces *make* to recompile *global.o*.

Maintaining a list of header files is so difficult that many people have developed complicated ways to automate the process. An increasing number of *make* extensions now find dependencies by running the C preprocessor on source files and checking the resulting **#include** directives. Some of these programs are described in Appendix B, *Popular Extensions*.

When we turn back to standard *make*, prospects for a solution look less attractive. Certainly, plenty of programmers over the years have devised schemes of varying sophistication. You may well come across one in some source distribution, in the form of a dummy target called *depend*. It generally contains a comment with the warning DO NOT DELETE THIS LINE, and uses that comment in a complicated, automated process that ends in overwriting the description file with new contents. We do not recommend this practice.

Some C compilers (notably from BSD and Sun Microsystems, Inc.) contain a **–M** option that generates a list of dependencies suitable for inclusion in a description file. This permits a fairly robust, home-brewed method of generating dependencies. For an example, start with the following description file, named *basic.mk*. You might want to review the section on forced rebuilds in this chapter before continuing.

```
OBJS = parse.o search_file.o global.o find_token.o
SOURCES = ${OBJS:.o=.c}

parse: ${FRC}
        ${MAKE} "CFLAGS=${CFLAGS}" "FRC=${FRC}" makefile
        ${MAKE} "CFLAGS=${CFLAGS}" "FRC=${FRC}" ${OBJS}
        ${CC} ${LDFLAGS} -o $@ ${OBJS}

makefile : ${FRC}
        rm -f $@
        cp basic.mk $@
        echo '# Automatically-generated dependencies list:' >> $@
        ${CC} ${CFLAGS} -M ${SOURCES} >> $@
        chmod -w $@

force_rebuild :
```

From this description file, we are going to build the real *makefile* that is used for building programs.

```
$ make -f basic.mk makefile
rm -f makefile
cp basic.mk makefile
echo '# Automatically-generated dependencies list:' >> makefile
```

```
cc  -M parse.c search_file.c global.c find_token.c >> makefile
chmod -w makefile
```

If we look now at the new *makefile*, we see a list of dependencies that represent the output of the *cc* command. If any options had been passed in CFLAGS, and if these options had affected the header files included, such effects would be reflected in the dependency list.

```
OBJS = parse.o search_file.o global.o find_token.o
SOURCES = ${OBJS:.o=.c}

parse: ${FRC}
    ${MAKE} "CFLAGS=${CFLAGS}" "FRC=${FRC}" makefile
    ${MAKE} "CFLAGS=${CFLAGS}" "FRC=${FRC}" ${OBJS}
    ${CC} ${LDFLAGS} -o $@ ${OBJS}

makefile : ${FRC}
    cp basic.mk $@
    echo '# Automatically-generated dependencies list:' >> $@
    ${CC} ${CFLAGS} -M ${SOURCES} >> $@

force_rebuild :
# Automatically-generated dependencies list:
parse.o: parse.c
parse.o: ./parse.h
parse.o: /usr/include/stdio.h
parse.o: /usr/include/ctype.h
parse.o: /usr/include/string.h
parse.o: /usr/include/sys/stdtypes.h
search_file.o: search_file.c
search_file.o: ./parse.h
search_file.o: /usr/include/stdio.h
search_file.o: /usr/include/ctype.h
search_file.o: /usr/include/string.h
search_file.o: /usr/include/sys/stdtypes.h
    . . .
```

We can now build any object files or executable files we want using the *makefile*.

When you want to update your *makefile*, you must do so with a forced rebuild.

```
$ make -f basic.mk makefile FRC=force_rebuild
```

You can do this before a major product build, or any time that you know that header files have changed. There is no way to design an automatic rebuild of *makefile* into your regular build procedures—after all, the whole reason behind the dependency list is that *make* cannot tell when dependencies change. But as an alternative to the FRC convention, you could simply have *makefile* depend on all the source files and header files that are specific to your project:

```
makefile : ${SOURCES} parse.h
```

This leads to a lot of extra rebuilds, because *makefile* must be rebuilt every time a source file or *parse.h* changes.

Things get even worse if your compiler does not offer a –**M** option. You can try parsing the source files yourself through a shell script, but it's hard work with shaky results. A tool for discovering header-file dependencies must search each .**c** file for **#include** directives and convert them into dependency lines suitable for a description file. To be robust—in case anyone but you uses the tool—it should be able to handle any legal variation in the source file syntax and directory path names.

Finally, a truly sophisticated tool would perform the search iteratively—because header files typically include other header files—and recognize **#if** and related preprocessor directives. Putting together these requirements, one can see that the best hope lies in using the C preprocessor, which is basically the underpinnings of the –**M** option as well as every extension in Appendix B that generates dependencies. Some people have tried to do the job with pattern searchers like *grep* and *sed*, but they are nowhere near powerful or adaptable enough.

Global Definitions (include Statement)

(This feature is not available in all variants; see Appendix C for a way to check your system.)

As description files proliferate on a large project—usually one description file per directory in the source tree—the project team should think about collecting macro definitions and suffix rules in a single place, just as common preprocessor definitions get collected in header files. To support such consolidation, *make* provides an **include** statement. The format is:

```
include file
```

where the word **include** must begin the line and must be followed by a space or tab. No preceding spaces or tabs are allowed. Some implementations allow multiple filenames, separated by spaces or tabs. The effect of this statement is the same as simply writing all the lines from *file* into the current description file. In general, you should put an **include** statement at the beginning of each description file in a project, and then store any rules, entries, and macro definitions you want to share in *file*.

You can customize the description file by expressing *file* as a macro:

```
INCMK = inc.mk
include ${INCMK}
```

The definition of INCMK must precede the `include` statement. Now someone can substitute another file of definitions. For instance, a programmer could put the following lines in a file named */usr/fred/proj/tmp.mk* :

```
INCLUDES = /usr/include_tmp
TESTDIR = /tmp/fred
```

and then force *make* to use those definitions through the command,

```
$ make INCMK=/usr/fred/proj/tmp.mk
```

which overrides the definition of INCMK in the main description file. All this is hardly worthwhile for just a few definitions; the same effect could be accomplished with

```
$ make INCLUDES=/usr/include_tmp TESTDIR=/tmp/fred
```

but for large sets of macros the `include` feature is valuable.

If you put dependency lines in include files, remember that macros must be defined before the dependency lines that refer to them. In other words, if your include file contains a target like

```
install : ${EXECS}
    . . .
```

don't ask users to define EXECS in their individual description files. Any definition of EXECS that comes after the `include` statement will go unrecognized. The definition should be in at least one of the following places:

1. The include file itself, before the dependency line.

2. The user's description file, before the `include` statement.

3. The *make* command line.

4. The user's environment variables.

Distributed Files and NFS Issues

A project that spans multiple network nodes is extremely hard to manage, unless you have an environment like the Network File System (NFS) to create the illusion of a single file system. Without this, you are reduced to issuing a lot of remote file copy commands, and dealing with all the file duplication and general fragility that results.

Even NFS imitates a uniform file system imperfectly. System clocks sometimes differ slightly, and NFS may take a few minutes for a change to a file to be reflected in the last-modified time, as seen on remote systems. You can sometimes view this inconsistency directly. In the following example, the files were stored on one system, and their directory was mounted on another system where the commands were issued:

```
$ make tfunc.o
cc -O -c tfunc.c                    (make builds tfunc.o as usual)


                                    (edit tfunc.c)

$ make tfunc.o
`tfunc.o´ is up to date.            (file modification not yet seen)
$ ls -al
total 164
-rw-r--r--  1          12 Jul 16 16:30 tfunc.c
-rw-r--r--  1          80 Jul 16 16:30 tfunc.o


                                    (wait a few minutes)

$ make tfunc.o
cc -O -c  tfunc.c                   (file modification can be seen)
```

But this slight inconsistency is not likely to hurt you during real-life builds. Storing and building files on multiple systems is an indispensable element of modern development environments.

If you don't have a distributed file system, sharing files is a job in itself. Here is a small example that might give you a start if you are stuck in that situation. The description file uses the familiar *rcp* (remote copy) command to transfer .c files to another system, and defines a new suffix, .t, to record that the transfer took place. Whenever someone changes a .c file on the local system, the corresponding .t file becomes out of date. So if you later remake all .t files, the necessary source files will be transferred.

```
# Transfers .c source files to the remote system named buildsys

.SUFFIXES : .t        # tells make that the .c file was transferred
.c.t :
    rcp $< buildsys:/usr/build
    echo "Transferred $< to buildsys on \c" > $@
    date '+%d %h %y %H:%M' >> $@
```

The example above was just a proof of concept. It contained a hard-coded directory, and didn't bother to check whether the *rcp* command actually succeeded.

The following version is more complicated and tries to address those failings. It assumes that source files can lie anywhere in a tree whose root is */usr/src* on the local system. The *rcp* command transfers them to a corresponding directory under */usr/build* on the remote system. Chapter 4, *Commands*, can help you untangle the single long shell command that forms this entry, and see how the *rcp* exit status is checked.

```
.SUFFIXES : .t          # tells make that the .c file was transferred
.c.t :
    TARGET_DIR=`pwd | sed 's?/usr/src?/usr/build?'` ; \
    if \
        rcp $< buildsys:$$TARGET_DIR ; \
    then \
        echo "Transferred $< to buildsys:$$TARGET_DIR on \c" > $@ ; \
        date '+%d %h %y %H:%M' >> $@ ; \
    else \
        echo "Error trying to transfer $< to buildsys:$$TARGET_DIR" ; \
    fi
```

6

Command-line Usage and Special Targets

Description Filenames
Status Information and Debugging
Errors and File Deletion
The MAKEFLAGS Macro
Miscellaneous Features Affecting Defaults

As the previous chapters have shown, you can get *make* to act in almost any manner you want by means of the suffix rules, macro definitions, and entries of your description file. But in addition, *make* provides some powerful forms of global control through both command-line options and a collection of targets with special meanings. These are the subjects of this chapter.

Some features are quite useful for debugging (such as the **–n** option) or for inducing the necessary flexibility from *make* (the **–f** option and the `.SUFFIXES` target). But many of the features, such as the **–i** option (ignore errors) and **–t** option (touch without rebuilding), override the natural responses of *make* in potentially dangerous ways. Their use should be reserved for evenings and weekends.

For a complete quick-reference overview of *make* options and syntax rules, see Appendix A.

Description Filenames

The **–f** option allows you to specify a description file with a non-standard name. For example, the command,

```
$ make -f term.mk iomod
```

tells *make* to use *term.mk* as a description file while generating the target, *iomod*. It is a convention to use the **.mk** suffix on any description file that does not bear the default name *makefile* or *Makefile*. You can effectively combine multiple description files by using more than one *–f file* argument pair on the command line. Finally, if you give a hyphen as the name of your description file:

```
$ make -f - iomod ...
```

make will read the description file from the standard input. This can be helpful for time-saving, interactive experimentation while you are learning how *make* works. However, *make* will not actually perform the tasks you request until you type a CTRL-D, signifying end-of-file. This is because *make* always reads the entire description file before executing any commands.

If you invoke *make* recursively within a description file, the name of the file is not passed along automatically; you must repeat your **–f** option in the $\{MAKE\} command.

Status Information and Debugging

make normally echoes to the standard output (your terminal) each command line that it executes. If you use the **–n** option, then *make* echoes the commands, but does not actually execute them. Therefore, the following invocation,

```
$ make -n full_test disp ...
```

enables you to find out in just a second or two the current state of one or more dependency hierarchies—that is, one or more sets of related files. This invocation tells you how much work *make* will have to do in order to regenerate the targets.

By saving the output of *make –n* in a script, you can create a command file. Sometimes such a file proves useful when *make* gets interrupted part way through its task and you want to finish the task manually. For best results, you should create the script *before* running the *make* that fails.

Conversely, the command,

```
$ make -s full_test disp ...
```

executes all required commands, but does not echo them. You can achieve exactly the same effect by placing the following target anywhere in your description file:

```
.SILENT :
```

These features are global, applying to the entire build. To prevent a particular command from being echoed, place an at-sign (@) before the command:

```
target : comp.c
    cc -O comp.c
    @ echo "Done"
```

All commands are echoed when you use the **–n** option, even those beginning with @.

The **–q** (question) option instructs *make* to return a zero status code if the target files are up-to-date, and a non-zero status code if they are out-of-date. You can sometimes use this feature to good advantage when invoking *make* from a shell command script:

```
if
    make -q comp1 comp2
then
    echo 'No work needs to be done; targets up to date.'
else
    date >> $LOGFILE
    ...
fi
```

The **–t** (touch) option causes *make* to change the last-modified date of the target to the current date. This is a potentially dangerous option, inasmuch as it destroys *make*'s record of the previous relations between files. But **–t** can save you some time if you know that your changes to a prerequisite have no effect on the targets depending on it. For instance, if you add a comment to a source file or header file, your next *make* would normally rebuild all the object files and libraries that depend on it. You might save a lot of time by immediately "making" these targets with the **–t** option.

As described in Chapter 3, *Suffix Rules*, the **–p** option causes *make* to print out the complete set of macro definitions, suffixes, suffix rules, and description file entries. Much more detailed (and not necessarily understandable!) information results from the **–d** (debug) option. It displays messages showing how *make* traces dependencies and determines what files to use during the build. Chapter 7, *Troubleshooting*, discusses the output from this option.

Errors and File Deletion

make normally stops if any executed command returns a non-zero (error) exit code. Before quitting, however, it removes the current target it is making. The assumption here is that the target is probably in a partly finished state. If it were left in place, it would appear to be up to date in subsequent invocations of *make*, due to its now revised date of last modification.

If you invoke *make* with the –i option, or put the target

```
.IGNORE
```

in your description file, *make* continues regardless of any errors returned by commands. As discussed in Chapter 4, a safer practice is to place a hyphen before each individual command whose status you wish to ignore.

There may be occasions when you do not want the target removed upon occurrence of errors. The .PRECIOUS target allows you to specify any files you do not want destroyed. For example, the following description file entry

```
.PRECIOUS : out.x gen.x
```

prevents any of the named targets from being removed by *make*. This entry can occur anywhere in the description file.

The MAKEFLAGS Macro

make automatically defines a macro, MAKEFLAGS, that contains the command-line options given in the current invocation of *make*. BSD 4.3 uses the name MFLAGS. (See Appendix C for a way to check the macro used on your system.)

If MAKEFLAGS is supported, and you invoke *make* with the following command,

```
$ make -ksf target.mk target
```

then the description file entry,

```
target :
        echo ${MAKEFLAGS}
```

results in the output,

```
ks
```

The **-f**, **-p**, and **-r** options do not show up in the **MAKEFLAGS** macro. However, an unsolicited **-b** might appear. Most implementations of *make* turn on the **–b** option by default. This option was originally invented to support backward compatibility with earlier implementations of *make*, so that old description files would continue to work. Now the option is redundant.

Judging from conventional *make* documentation and source code, the intent is that *make* use the presence of a shell variable named **MAKEFLAGS** to set command-line options at startup time. The description file could also define **MAKEFLAGS** as an environment variable or a macro, and its current value would then affect recursive invocations of *make*.

However, existing implementations of *make* vary in their handling of **MAKEFLAGS**, and many refuse to allow any manipulation of flags by the user, either from the environment or in a macro definition. In some cases, such a redefinition could even abort otherwise correct executions of *make*. We recommend that you do not manipulate **MAKEFLAGS** directly.

Miscellaneous Features Affecting Defaults

The **–r** option has an effect similar to **.SUFFIXES** without a suffix list: it causes *make* to ignore the default rules. See Chapter 3 for a discussion of default rules and when they should be ignored.

Commands associated with the **.DEFAULT** target are executed if a file must be made but there are no relevant description file entries or suffix rules. For example:

```
.DEFAULT :
    ls -l
    echo "No targets to make"
```

The **.DEFAULT** target can be a crude way to retrieve files from a public place. Thus, if a copy of every source file for a project is stored in */usr/src*, the following entry copies over each file that you need during a build.

```
.DEFAULT :
    cp /usr/src/$@ .
```

7

Troubleshooting

Debugging a Build (-d Option)
Syntax Errors
Don't Know How to Make
Target Up to Date
Command Not Found, or Cannot Load
Syntax Errors in Multi-line Commands
Inconsistent Lines, or Too Many Lines
Unrecognized Macros
Default Rules Ignored

The messages issued by *make* can prove bewildering until you become familiar with the way it operates. A few brief messages cover a wide variety of possible errors. Furthermore, *make* can do very puzzling things without reporting any error, because it believes it has done what you asked it to do.

Debugging a Build (-d Option)

If you have trouble figuring out why *make* has chosen to take certain actions during a build—what made it choose certain suffix rules, rebuild certain files, and leave other files untouched—try running *make* with the **–d** option. As *make* goes through each dependency check and builds targets, it displays descriptive messages.

System V *make*, unfortunately, displays the information produced by **–d** in the form of variables and terse messages that are most useful to a programmer debugging the *make* source code. We will try to clarify the most valuable elements of the output here. Some modern variants—notably those from GNU and from Sun Microsystems—display messages that are more self-explanatory.

Each macro and environment variables is displayed with an `envflg` flag and a `noreset` flag. The string

```
envflg = 0
```

indicates that the definition of corresponding variable comes from within *make*—that is, either from an internal definition or from the description file. The string

```
envflg = 1
```

signifies that the definition comes from your command line or your shell environment.

In Chapter 2, *Macros*, we saw that command-line variable definitions always override the description file, and that the **–e** option forces your shell environment to override the description file. In the **–d** output, the string

```
noreset = 0
```

means that *make* can override the definition later. This string appears next to environment variables when you invoke *make* without **–e**. The string

```
noreset = 1
```

means the current definition cannot be overridden. This string appears next to environment variables when you run *make* with **–e**. `noreset` is always 0 for internally defined macros and 1 for the variables that you set on the command line.

When *make* starts checking targets to see whether they are up to date, you see a line like

doname(*file*, *level*)

for each *file* in the chain of dependencies, as *make* searches backward. The *level* starts at zero for the targets that you specify on the command line, and increments by one for each step backward in the chain. The last-modified time of each file is displayed as raw UNIX time in the form TIME(*file*)=*time*. If the number displayed for a target is lower than that of its prerequisite, the target is out of date.

Unfortunately, *make* does not pass the **–d** option to recursively-invoked makes; so you may lose some of the information trail as the recursive makes execute.

Syntax Errors

The most trivial, but most frustrating, message received by novice *make* users is one indicating some kind of syntax problem with their description file. Typically it looks like this:

```
Make: Must be a separator on rules line 3.  Stop.
```

and often there is nothing visibly wrong with the offending line. Usually, the problem is that you have begun the line with a space instead of a tab. *make* requires that you use a tab as the first character of each command line.

Another invisible error is a line consisting only of a tab, in a place where no command is allowed. This generates the following message:

```
Make: line 3: syntax error. Stop.
```

You can easily introduce a problem by editing a line that ends with a backslash. Make sure there are no spaces or tabs after the backslash. Also make sure that the last line of a command or macro definition does *not* end with a backslash.

General problems with parsing lead to errors like:

```
Bad character { (octal 173), line 3
```

which means you have to look at how you used a { on line 3. In this case, a dependency line referred to {FILES} instead of ${FILES} (a missing dollar sign, which is an easy mistake to make).

Some syntax errors issue from the shell that *make* invokes. As one often finds on UNIX systems, it can be hard to tell where an error message is coming from.

Don't Know How to Make

If you enter

```
$ make reqtarg
```

and receive the following in return:

```
Make:  Don't know how to make reqtarg.  Stop.
```

it means you have neither a dependency line naming *reqtarg* as a target, nor a suffix rule that can build *reqtarg* from any file in the current directory. Aside from simple misspellings, a common cause is that you have a suffix rule to build *reqtarg*, but no prerequisite with the required name. For instance, if you are trying to build *trac.c* and have defined a **.x.c** rule, this error message means that *trac.x* does not exist.

You will receive a similar message if some specified prerequisite of the target fulfills the same conditions. For example, suppose you have the entries,

```
reqtarg :  main.o func.o
    ${CC} main.o func.o

main.o : main.c
    ${CC} -c -DREQ main.c
```

but do not have any way to build *func.o*. Since *main.o* comes first, *make* will build it successfully, but will then fail when searching for a way to build *func.o*:

```
$ make reqtarg
cc -c -DREQ main.c
Make.  Don't know how to make func.o.  Stop.
```

The most subtle problems arise when you use built-in suffix rules without providing required source files. For instance, *reqtarg* will build successfully in the previous example if the current directory contains a file named *func.c*. But if someone removes or renames the C source file, *make* will search for some other file from which it can build an object file—a Fortran source file, a *yacc* source file, and so on—and finally give up with the above error message when it finds none.

Finally, the message above could simply mean that your description file is missing. Perhaps you used a name other than *makefile* or *Makefile*; in that case, be sure to specify the name in a **–f** option.

Target Up to Date

If you try to build a target such as *reqtarg* and *make* reports:

```
`reqtarg` is up-to-date.
```

it means that all of the following are true:

- *reqtarg* is an existing file in the current directory.

- *reqtarg* has no prerequisites specified in a description file entry. (It might not even have a description file entry.)

- No file exists that is newer than *reqtarg*, and which can be used to build *reqtarg* according to the suffix rules.

If you depart from standard build procedures, you can easily confuse *make* into missing dependencies. For instance, if you store sources outside the current directory, you have to use one of the techniques shown in Chapter 5, *Project Management*, to force *make* to look in the right place for each one. If it cannot find a source file, *make* will conclude that any existing object file is up-to-date. Similar problems occur with hidden dependencies, such as when you change a **.h** header file but forget to list it explicitly in dependency line.

Sometimes a target has no associated prerequisites. Normally, you use such a target to explicitly and unambiguously run a set of commands. For example, you might have an entry to print your program:

```
print :
     pr *.c > printer_output
     lpr printer_output
     rm -f printer_output
```

and indeed, a **make print** command should inevitably execute these lines. But suppose somebody happened to create a file named *print*, not realizing that you had reserved that word as a target? If such a file exists, *make* will simply tell you that it is up-to-date, regardless of any other considerations.

Command Not Found, or Cannot Load

If you see the message,

cmmd: Command not found.

or

Make: Cannot load *cmmd*. Stop.

it means that your file contains a command named *cmmd* that does not exist. The first message is a standard shell diagnostic, and means that *make* invoked the shell to execute the command. The second message is from *make* itself, indicating that the command contained no shell metacharacters and was therefore invoked directly from *make*. The probable causes are the same in either case.

First, are you using the right shell, and is **cmmd** an alias? The most reliable way to use *make* is to place the line,

SHELL = /bin/sh

in every description file, and not to use aliases.

Second, does your path include the command? Your PATH environment variable is passed to the shells invoked by *make*.

Finally, have you used a complicated command that covers more than one line of the description file? Make sure to place a backslash at the end of each line that is meant to be continued. Otherwise, *make* starts the following line as a new command. Here is a problematic entry, which ought to have a backslash after the CFLAGS argument:

```
OBJECTS = main.o io.o diddec.o

make_dec :
    make dec "CFLAGS=${CFLAGS}"
    "OBJECTS=${OBJECTS}"
```

and the resulting output, indicating that *make* executed the OBJECTS line separately:

```
make x dec "CFLAGS=-O"
(commands building dec)
    . . .
"OBJECTS=main.o io.o diddec.o"
sh: OBJECTS=main.o io.o diddec.o: not found
*** Error code 1

Stop.
```

If *make* fails because it cannot start a new shell:

```
couldn't load shell
```

this means either that you've specified a non-existent pathname in your SHELL command, or that you are trying to start more processes than your system allows.

You are very unlikely to run up against any internal limits in *make*. It does have some hard-coded buffer sizes and similar limits, but they are set so high that you are practically guaranteed never to exceed them unless you generate extremely long lines through some automated procedure. The limits depend both on the implementation's definitions and on internal parsing rules, so we cannot try to list them here. Examples of limits include the length of a macro definition, the length of a command, the number of characters in the $? list, and the number of files you can use as targets and prerequisites during a build. The standard advice—should you actually exceed one of these limits—is to break a long dependency line into several short ones, or to break the entire description file into smaller files tied together by recursive makes.

Syntax Errors in Multi-line Commands

If you use commands that contain nested commands, such as *if* constructs from the shell, check your use of semicolons and backslashes rigorously. Chapter 4 has a few examples to help. You must avoid the complementary errors of breaking the construct too early, and of joining two commands that must be separated by a semicolon. For instance, the following:

```
directory_make :
    for subdir in ${DIRS} ; \
    do \
        cd $${subdir} ; make all
    done
```

produces the error

```
sh: syntax error at line 3: `end of file´ unexpected
```

because you ended the *for* command prematurely. The cure is to add both a semicolon and a backslash at the end of the *make all* command. A complementary error is to join two commands together:

```
mkdir :
    if [ ! -z $"{TMPDIR}" ] \
    then \
        mkdir ${TMPDIR} ; \
    fi
```

which produces the error

```
sh: syntax error at line 4: `fi´ unexpected
```

The square brackets (which some shells accept in lieu of a *test*(1) command) represent a separate command. Therefore, the closing bracket must be followed by both a semicolon and a backslash.

Other common errors include "unrecognized command" (because you forgot to continue a line with a backslash) and the simple "syntax error" (which might be caused by putting white space after the final backslash). If the lines of a shell command contain an embedded comment, the comment must also end with a backslash.

Strange error messages can appear if you write commands for one shell, and *make* invokes another. To avoid this annoying mistake, set the SHELL macro to */bin/sh* and write all your commands using the Bourne shell.

Inconsistent Lines, or Too Many Lines

A family of *make* messages reports duplicate entries for targets. It is quite common, and legal, to put a target on several dependency lines. But you must consistently use one colon or two colons on these dependency lines.

If the dependency lines contain one colon, only one of the lines can be followed by commands. Those commands are always used to build the target, and the other dependency lines exist just to tell *make* when the target needs to be rebuilt.

You can use two colons on dependency lines when you need to use different commands for different prerequisites, but this situation is rare. It generally occurs for libraries, as described in Chapter 3.

If you put commands under multiple dependency lines (of the single-colon type) you get error messages like:

```
too many command lines for `target´
```

The original term for a dependency line was *rules line*, and you see this term in an error message if you specify the same target on single-colon and double-colon dependency lines:

```
inconsistent rules lines for `target´
```

Here's a message you're not likely to encounter, but if you ever do, it can give you a bit of a shock:

```
$! nulled, predecessor cycle
```

No, this is not the strange by-product of string concatenation; it is a hard-coded message that someone thought up and wrote into the source code. You can elicit it if *file.x* depends on *file.z* and *file.z* depends on *file.x*, perhaps because you got mixed up while writing suffix rules.

Unrecognized Macros

You are probably used to typing shell variables like $HOME without curly braces. But *make* macros need parentheses or curly braces for any macro longer than one character. If you forget this requirement, a command like

```
for file in $OBJECTS ...
```

will likely evaluate to

```
for file in BJECTS
```

which is pretty easy to diagnose: *make* looked for a macro named $O, couldn't find one, substituted a null string, and reproduced the rest of the string literally. You can encounter this problem if you plug shell scripts right into description files. The same error on a dependency line:

```
prog : $OBJECTS
```

produces the error message:

```
Make:  Don't know how to make BJECTS.  Stop.
```

A related problem comes from trying to use a shell variable without doubling the dollar sign. The entry,

```
lint :
    for file in *.c ; \
    do \
        lint ${file} >> lint.output ; \
    done
```

will produce a faulty *lint* command. As Chapter 4 explains, `file` is a shell variable, and therefore must be referred to as `$$file` or `$${file}`. The entry shown above refers to a macro, and since your file is not likely to define `file` as a macro, *make* substitutes a null string.

If macros refer to one another in a circular fashion:

```
FILE = /usr/${INCLUDES}
INCLUDES = ${FILE}
```

then executing *make* yields the message

```
Make: infinitely recursive macro?. Stop.
```

The reason for the question mark is that *make* doesn't establish definitively whether you have a circular definition; it simply loops for a long time while expanding the macro and then gives up. A circular definition could cause some variants to abort with a core dump.

Remember that you cannot treat your description file as a program, redefining macros on the fly as if they were variables or assembler symbols. Define each macro once, before the dependency lines—that is, before your list of targets. This is because *make* evaluates the macros on each dependency line during its first pass through the description file, and cannot use any macro definitions that follow the dependency line. Macros in `include` statements have the same restriction.

The use of backslashes to continue a long macro is a common source of syntax errors. Within macros, *make* is particularly ruthless with white space, stripping away newlines as well as spaces and tabs after each backslash.

Default Rules Ignored

Suppose there is a file *main.c* in the current directory. Consider first this description file entry, with no associated commands:

```
main.o : defs.h
```

This is a perfectly reasonable entry, letting *make* know that *main.o* must be rebuilt if the *defs.h* header file changes. Following default suffix rules, *make* recompiles *main.c* to make *main.o*. But if you put a command under the entry, such as:

```
main.o : defs.h
        echo "main.o remade"
```

this command overrides the default suffix rule. Now, *make* simply executes the *echo* command and does nothing else.

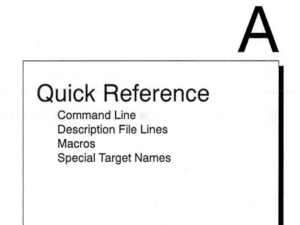

Quick Reference

Command Line
Description File Lines
Macros
Special Target Names

make [**-f** *descfile*] [*options*] [*targets*] [*macro definitions*]

Options, targets, and macro definitions can be in any order. You can combine several options after a single hyphen, as in **–fsn**. The format of a macro definition is:

   name=string

Standard options are:

–b   Accept description files from previous implementations of *make*.

–d   Debug mode—print detailed information about internal flags and the last-modified times of files.

–e   Let environment variables override macro definitions inside description files.

-f   Following argument is a description file. If the argument is a hyphen, the standard input is used. You can pass multiple –f options, specifying one description file per option, and these files will be concatenated.

-i   Ignore error codes. Same as .IGNORE: in description file.

-k   Error terminates work on current branch of hierarchy, but not on other branches.

-n   Echo command lines, but do not execute them. Even lines beginning with @ are echoed.

-p   Print out macro definitions, suffixes, suffix rules, and explicit description file entries.

-q   Return zero or non-zero status, depending on whether the target file is or is not up to date.

-r   Do not use the default rules.

-s   Do not echo command lines. Same as .SILENT: in description file.

-t   Touch target files (making them appear up to date), without executing any other commands.

Description File Lines

Any line can be followed by a pound sign (#) and comment. Blank lines are ignored. Any line ending in a backslash (\) is considered to continue on the next line of the description file. All the white space before the backslash and at the beginning of the following line is compressed to a single space.

Dependency line: *targets* :[:] [*prerequisites*] [; [*command*]]

Specifies that *targets* depend on *prerequisites*. Targets and prerequisites must be separated by spaces or tabs. Spaces before and after colons are optional. No tab is permitted before *targets*. The double colon allows you to specify the same target on multiple dependency lines, each of which is followed by commands. Target names should contain only letters, digits, periods, and underlines. Other characters might or might not be accepted by your version of *make*, depending on its parsing rules. After a semicolon, a command can appear.

Suffix rule: *.suffix*[*.suffix*]   **:** [**:**]

>   Specifies that files ending with the first *suffix* can be prerequisites of files
>   that have the same names but end with the second *suffix* (or no suffix, if
>   the second suffix is omitted). No spaces are permitted between the suf-
>   fixes. Anything after a colon is ignored. The double colon has no effect;
>   it is permitted because it is consistent with dependency lines. Suffixes
>   should contain only letters, digits, periods, and underlines. Other char-
>   acters might or might not be accepted by your version of *make*, depend-
>   ing on its parsing rules.

Command: tab [- @] *command*

>   Specifies a command to be executed when building a target. The tab
>   must be present. Optional spaces and tabs can follow. No line can start
>   with a tab unless a command follows. A hyphen (–) causes *make* to
>   ignore any error returned (non-zero exit status). An at-sign (@)
>   suppresses echoing of the line, except for runs with the **–n** option.

Macro definition: *name* = *string*

>   Assigns *string* to *name*. Optional spaces are allowed before *name*, but
>   the line must not begin with a tab. Optional spaces and tabs are allowed
>   before and after the equal sign (=), and are stripped off. If the *string*
>   contains a backslash followed by a newline, *make* continues the *string*
>   on the following line. One space is substituted for the backslash and
>   newline; in addition, all the white space before the backslash and at the
>   beginning of the following text (including newlines) is compressed to a
>   single space. Everything else in *string* becomes part of the definition,
>   including any trailing white space or double or single quotes. Macro
>   names should contain only letters, digits, and underlines. Other charac-
>   ters might or might not be accepted by your version of *make*, depending
>   on its parsing rules.

Include statement: `include` *file*

>   (Not available in all variants.) Reads and evaluates the contents of *file*
>   as if it were part of the description file. The file can be expressed as a
>   macro, if that macro is defined before the `include` statement. The
>   word `include` must be located at the very beginning of the line and
>   must be followed by a space or tab. Some implementations allow multi-
>   ple filenames, separated by spaces or tabs.

Macros

This section lists macros that have special meanings to *make*, and general syntax rules governing macro references.

Internal Macros

$?   The list of prerequisites that have been changed more recently than the current target. Can be used only in normal description file entries, not suffix rules.

$@   The name of the current target, except in description file entries for making libraries, where it becomes the library name. Can be used in both normal description file entries and suffix rules.

$$@   The name of the current target. Can be used only to the right of the colon in dependency lines.

$<   The name of the current prerequisite that has been modified more recently than the current target. Can be used only in suffix rules and the **.DEFAULT** entry.

$*   The name—without the suffix—of the current prerequisite that has been modified more recently than the current target. Can be used only in suffix rules.

$%   The name of the corresponding **.o** file when the current target is a library module. Can be used in both normal description file entries and suffix rules.

Macro Modifiers

(Not available in all variants.)

D   The directory portion of any internal macro except **$?**. Valid uses are ${@D}, $${@D}, ${<D}, ${*D}, and ${%D}.

F   The file portion of any internal macro except **$?**. Valid uses are ${@F}, $${@F}, ${<F}, ${*F}, and ${%F}.

Macro String Substitution

(Not available in all variants.)

${macro:*s1***=***s2***}**
Evaluates to the current definition of **${macro}**, after substituting the string *s2* for every occurrence of *s1* that occurs either immediately before a blank or tab, or at the end of the macro definition.

Macros with Special Handling

SHELL Determines which shell is used to interpret commands. If this macro is not defined in the description file, some implementations take the shell from the user's environment, as with other macros. Other implementations set SHELL to */bin/sh* by default, at least for top-level makes.

VPATH (Not available in all variants.) Specifies a list of directories that *make* searches to find prerequisites, if they are not in the current directory.

Special Target Names

.DEFAULT: Commands associated with this target are executed if *make* cannot find any description file entries or suffix rules with which to build a requested target.

.IGNORE: Ignore error codes. Same as the **–i** option.

.PRECIOUS: Files you specify for this target are not removed when you send a signal (such as interrupt) that aborts *make*, or when a command line in your description file returns an error.

.SILENT: Execute commands but do not echo them. Same as the **–s** option.

.SUFFIXES: The "prerequisites" associated with this target are suffixes that become significant for *make* and can become associated with suffix rules. Without accompanying suffixes, this target nullifies the existing suffix list. Suffixes must be separated by spaces or tabs.

B

Popular Extensions

mk and nmake
GNU make
imake
makedepend
shape
Parallel and Distributed Implementations

Users of *make* have developed a number of gripes and wish-list items over the years. Given the utility's powerful basic concepts—dependency analysis, macros, rule-driven command generation—there is a lot of room in *make* for expansion. The standard implementation discussed in this book is itself a product of evolution, and this evolution continues unabated both at Bell Labs and elsewhere.

In this appendix, we describe a few of the products that are publicly available and free of charge. We do not judge or rate these efforts. We present them so that you know they exist and can choose to learn more about them. Even if you never use them, you can learn a lot from this appendix, concerning the directions in which UNIX systems and the field of project management are headed.

As you read about the extensions, you will see that most of them simply formalize the techniques that users discovered and built around *make* over the years. A few extensions remove arbitrary restrictions in *make* or broaden its current abilities; these represent clear improvements, but do not attack the most pressing problems. Of the extensions that do have high ambitions, most rely on integrating *make* with other standard elements of UNIX systems, and therefore suffer from any incompatibilities and restrictions that result.

mk and nmake

Over the past decade or so, a number of computer scientists at AT&T have extended and modernized *make*. Their goal is to solve the problems that have long been known to programmers working on large, multi-versioned products—problems such as those discussed in Chapter 5, *Project Management*.

Since the extensions have been incremental, and tend to accompany experiments and discoveries concerning other aspects of project management, there is no single grand idea behind these tools. Instead, they embody a collection of useful innovations in different areas, adding up to a management tool that is significantly more sophisticated than *make*. Over the years, two of the tools have filtered out into the user community and received a positive response: Andrew Hume's *mk* and Glenn Fowler's *nmake*. Since *nmake* seems to be more comprehensive, we will briefly describe its most valuable features here.

The *nmake* search strategy assumes an extremely modular directory structure. Some directories should be devoted to source files (.c), some to header files (.h), some to libraries (.a), and so on. Such a directory structure is already quite common on large programming projects. With this in place, the programming team can tell *nmake* where to find files by assigning directories to the targets .SOURCE.c, .SOURCE.h, .SOURCE.a, and so on. There is even a special way to specify a search path for description files.

Thus, the notion of a viewpath, discussed in Chapter 5, *Project Management*, has been greatly extended and refined in *nmake*. It still recognizes the VPATH macro as well.

Predefined suffix rules now encompass multiple levels. The most general level holds base rules, which represent fairly universal operations on UNIX systems like building .o files from .c files. The next level is global rules, which change from project to project; these meet the sort of need for which standard *make* offers include files. At the top level lie user rules, defined in individual description files. The user rules override global rules where their domains overlap, and both types override base rules.

To clarify further how each target is built, *nmake* forces the user to indicate on each dependency line whether to build the target using predefined rules or explicit, user-supplied assertions. (*nmake* uses the term **assertion** where this book uses **entry**.) The syntax for defining rules has been extended, to allow more flexible pattern-matching than *make* suffix rules. A percent sign represents the string to be matched, and it can be delimited by periods at both the front and at the back. Thus, you can use s.%.c to represent an SCCS file of C source code.

One of the most popular *make* extensions is to scan the contents of source files to find dependencies on header files. This feature has been built into *nmake*.

Many *nmake* innovations are tailored to C programming, rather than being generalized to a theoretical ideal of a "build process." This approach is reasonable given the dominance of C programming in projects involving UNIX systems. At any rate, with a small amount of effort, the *nmake* developers have created similar extensions to support other programming environments. They have even tailored some extensions for *troff*, a gesture that can certainly be appreciated by technical writers (as well as any programmer who has to write a report, specification, or proposal).

Other extensions that contribute to efficiency and flexibility in *nmake* include:

- Supplying the missing links in backward chaining. Thus, if you want to rebuild an **.o** file and *nmake* finds the corresponding **.y** file, it can figure out what to do from its built-in **.y-to-.c** and **.c-to-.o** rules. Standard *make* has an additional **.y-to-.o** rule, because it cannot supply the missing link in the absence of a **.c** file.

- Maintaining state information for rebuilds in state variables (*nmake* uses the term **variable** instead of **macro**). The variables that you supply on the *nmake* command line, such as compiler options, are preserved in a special file named *makefile.ms* and re-used on subsequent builds. This file also stores other information about prerequisite files to improve speed.

- More sophisticated macro assignment, including the ability to tie changes in one macro to changes in another.

- Improved speed through compiled description files (*makefile.so*), parallelism, and the use of a coshell (an operating system extension developed at AT&T that represents an answer to the multi-threaded processes used in some other systems).

- Execution of multiple lines in a single shell, so that you can include shell scripts without the error-prone use of semicolons and backslashes discussed in Chapter 4.

- Built-in flow control statements, which act like an assembly language's macro processor.

- Finer control on an assertion-by-assertion basis over such specifications as `.IGNORE` (renamed `.DONTCARE`) and `.PRECIOUS`.

- More internal macros, such as $! to represent all files that are prerequisites of the current target.

- Abstracted actions. You can define a set of commands once and then invoke it with parameters from a variety of places through a `.USE` attribute, like calling a subroutine from a program.

Creator: Glenn Fowler, AT&T.

Available from: *nmake* has been distributed by AT&T in a package of utilities called the AT&T Toolkit.

Documentation: The information in this book was drawn from a presentation at the *UNIX Challenge '91* conference. Various other papers on *mk* and *nmake* have been circulated.

GNU make

Like most of the utilities released by the Free Software Foundation as part of the GNU project, its *make* is an emulation of the standard version written totally from the ground up (a kind of clean-room engineering), along with some common extensions and other new features that the creator decided were valuable. The major extensions include:

- Conditional evaluation of rules and macros, similar to conditional compilation in the C preprocessor. For instance, a description file can check whether a user assigned **yes** to the macro **DEBUG**, and if so, assign the value **–g** to **CFLAGS**. This addresses the problem of dynamically controlling *make*'s activities, which requires recursion in standard *make*.

- Parallel execution. See the last section of this appendix.

- Functions for manipulating strings and macros, so you can join macros, extract words, and perform other such manipulations. For instance `${firstword $(OBJS)}` evaluates to the first filename in the macro `$(OBJS)`, while `${dir $(OBJS)}` evaluates to the directory portions of the filenames in `$(OBJS)`.

- A more sophisticated viewpath (VPATH) feature, letting you tie particular directories to particular sets of files instead of forcing *make* to search the same series of directories for all files.

- A broader form of pattern-matching in filenames, so you can operate on other strings besides suffixes. A percent sign (%) embedded in a filename is a wildcard that can match any string of characters.

- Canned command sequences, which let you assign a symbol to a series of commands and then refer to them later by symbol. For instance, you can define `run-yacc` as a sequence of commands handling *yacc* and its output. This sequence can then be included under many targets, simplifying maintenance.

- Supplying the missing links in backward chaining, as *mk* and *nmake* do.

- Built-in rules for a number of extra languages, including C++ and Pascal.

- Support for RCS (Revision Control System), a free utility that performs the same general function as *sccs*, and is also available from the Free Software Foundation.

Creator:	Roland McGrath, Free Software Foundation.
Available from:	Free Software Foundation, Inc. 675 Massachusetts Ave. Cambridge, Massachusetts 02139 USA Available by anonymous *ftp* from `prep.ai.mit.edu`, in a subdirectory of */pub/gnu*, and from numerous other sites publicized by the Free Software Foundation.
Documentation:	GNU *make* comes with GNU's usual texinfo online documentation—in this case, a very thorough and well-written discussion.

imake

This is a preprocessor for *make* description files. It offers programming teams a great deal of flexibility in determining what *make* does for different operating systems, software releases, and so on. Although *imake* (which stands for "include make") has been used on a variety of projects, most of the computer field knows it through its use as a distribution and build tool for the X Window System.

By doing an extra level of processing that *make* cannot do itself, *imake* tries to solve all the problems of large projects listed at the beginning of Chapter 5, *Project Management*. *make* users have traditionally attacked such problems by passing their description files through some sort of filter, and *imake* simply formalizes that activity. The main filter that it uses is the C preprocessor.

Imagine that you have an enormous tree of source directories under the top-level *mit/clients* directory, as shown below. Each directory contains at least one *make* description file, and within each description file you have to define CFLAGS, CPP, LIBDIR, and a number of other macros.

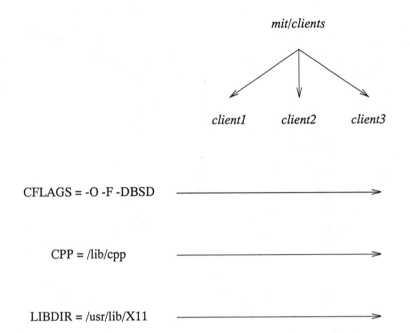

Although macro definitions are used in the figure, the same issues arise for standard directories, operating system features, and any other differences between systems that emerge in a program's source code or in the build process. The X Window System is supported even by many non-UNIX systems, all using the same source directories. So the difficulties of maintaining build procedures are probably the most formidable in the history of the computer field.

To use *imake*, the project team has to categorize every difference between systems and assign it to a variable. For instance, in the X distribution, DefaultCCOptions is a catch-all for C compiler options, while HasSockets indicates whether the system supports Berkeley socket communications.

After defining dozens of such variables, the team can set up templates for description files (using the name *Imakefile*). The variables, such as `DefaultCCOptions` and `HasSockets`, are defined themselves in site-specific files like *sun.cf* or *ultrix.cf*. If we were to use the figure shown earlier to reflect all the relationships, it would extend into three or four dimensions.

An invocation of *imake* searches for all relevant files and passes each *Imakefile* through the C preprocessor with the proper definitions. The files also pass through some other utilities, and undergo some clean-up in *imake* itself. Part of the user's job along the way is to run them through the *makedepend* tool described in the next section of this appendix. The result is a fairly conventional description file, which *imake* can save for later or pass immediately to standard *make*.

The C preprocessor is quite a powerful tool, as programmers have long known. For instance, *imake* defines macros such as

```
InstallProgram(program,dest) ...
```

and the description file comes out of the C preprocessor with a set of entries installing various programs in various destinations. Nothing is magic, however; this impressive transformation requires special syntax rules and postprocessing by *imake*. With all its power, *imake* remains a hostage to the peculiarities and inconsistencies of the tools that it ties together.

Creators: Todd Brunhoff, Tektronix and MIT Project Athena; Jim Fulton, MIT X Consortium.

Available from: MIT X Consortium
545 Technology Square, Room 217
Cambridge, Massachusetts 02139
USA

Available by anonymous *ftp* from `expo.lcs.mit.edu` in a subdirectory of */pub*, and from numerous other sites.

Documentation: For a tool that is so widely distributed, *imake* remains extraordinarily underdocumented. We do not hope to ameliorate the situation with this brief introduction, but only to give you an idea of how *imake* fits into the tasks normally assigned to *make*.

Various authors have tackled bits and pieces of *imake*, but they fail to separate the tool's general use from the eccentricities of its employment in the distribution of the X Window System. No well-paced user documentation yet exists. What does exist is:

- *An Imake Tutorial*, by Mark Moraes, in the *mit/contrib* directory of the X Window System release.

- *Using Imake to Configure the X Window System Version 11, Release 4*, by Paul Dubois (e-mail address: dubois@primate.wisc.edu), available by anonymous *ftp* in the directory ⁻*ftp/pub/imake-stuff* at:

  indri.primate.wisc.edu (128.104.230.11)

- An *imake* manual page in the */mit/config* directory of the X Window System release, which also contains various accompanying release notes.

makedepend

Chapter 5, *Project Management*, described how programmers extract their programs' hidden dependencies on header files. This requires some tool that searches source files for **#include** directives and transforms the list of .h filenames into dependency lines, eventually writing these into the *make* description file. The process has reached the state of high art in a program called *makedepend*.

As we described in the previous section, *makedepend* is a companion of *imake*. Many people also use *makedepend* by itself. It contains just about all the sophistication one could ask for in such a tool: automatic determination of standard directories, recursive searches through included header files, sensitivity to your choice of C compiler options, and recognition of the C preprocessor directives that affect included files (that is, **#if** and other constructs controlling conditional compilation).

Creators: Todd Brunhoff, Tektronix and MIT Project Athena.

Available from: MIT X Consortium
                        545 Technology Square, Room 217
                        Cambridge, Massachusetts 02139
                        USA

                        Available by anonymous *ftp* from **expo.lcs.mit.edu** in a subdirectory of */pub* and from numerous other sites.

Documentation: A *mkdepend* manual page resides in the *mit/util* directory of the X Window System release, and the utility is discussed somewhat in the documentation listed earlier under *imake*.

shape

This toolkit is an ambitious replacement for both *make* and *sccs*. It embodies a version control system and the *shape* program itself for building targets. Because version control is integrated into the toolkit, *shape* has full access to all versions of the source files.

The *shape* toolkit lets you specify explicitly the attributes that tend to be important on large projects—such as the development state for each source version, which system the release runs on, which compiler options and C preprocessor symbols you have used to compile each source file, and so on. You can also associate these attributes to particular versions of files, and ask *shape* to retrieve those versions during its builds.

Like *make*, *shape* uses a description file called *Shapefile*, which has some parts similar to a standard *makefile* and a number of extensions. *shape* is upwardly compatible to *make*, in the sense that it is able to interpret a standard *makefile*.

Suppose that your development cycle is characterized by a set of practices:

1. You compile with the GNU *gcc* compiler.

2. You use the **–g** option for debugging purposes.

3. You link with some special functions maintained by your team in the file *local.o*, to handle some peculiarities at your development site.

When you release your product, you employ some very different practices:

1. You compile with your system's proprietary *cc* compiler.

2. You compile with **–O** to optimize the object files, and link with **–s** to strip the executable file.

3. You omit *local.o* from your object files and let the linker resolve references from the standard libraries instead.

To organize these shifting requirements, *shape* provides a framework for creating and keeping track of multiple variants of a target, built by different compilers, different options, and different object files. A new construct, a *variant class*, holds the different values that you want macros to take on during different builds. For the present example, you would set the macro holding the compiler's filename in the **compiler** variant class and the CFLAGS in the **quality** variant class. Of course, you can create your own classes, too.

The requirements just listed above would look something like this in your description file:

```
#% VARIANT-SECTION
vclass quality ::= (test, final)

test:
    CFLAGS = -g
    LDFLAGS = -g
final:
    CFLAGS = -O
    LDFLAGS = -s

vclass compiler ::= (pcc, gcc).

pcc:
    CC=cc
gnu:
    CC=gcc -traditional -W

test_objects:
    OBJS = $(RELOBJS) local.o

release_objects:
    OBJS = $(RELOBJS)
#% END-VARIANT-SECTION
```

You can activate all the variants you want in your dependency lines:

```
RELOBJS = find_token.o global.o parse.o search_file.o

test : +test +gnu +test_objects $(OBJS)

install : +final +pcc +release_objects $(OBJS)
```

In addition to the variant section, a *shape* description file can have a rule section that controls which version of the source file is used in each build. The selection is determined by the attributes tagged to each version in the version control system, such as the development state or version number.

shape formalizes the method shown in Chapter 5, *Project Management*, in which programmers keep separate locations for files built with different compiler options. The version control system stores object files as well as source files, and preserves information on the options used to create them so that it can fetch the right versions when needed.

In summary, *shape* offers two major extensions to standard make: full access to the version control system, and the ability to manage any number of attributes for each version. The variant classes replace the welter of macros and –D compiler options that you are responsible for tracking when you use standard *make*.

Creators: Wilfried Koch, Andreas Lampen, Axel Mahler, Ulrich Pralle, and Wolfgang Obst, Technical University of Berlin.

Available from: Technical University of Berlin
"shape"
Sekr. FR 5-6
Franklinstr. 28/29
D-1000 Berlin 10, Federal Republic of Germany
E-mail address:
  shape@cs.tu-berlin.de

Documentation: The software comes with a tutorial, which includes examples, and a set of manual pages. Articles on *shape* appear in the following professional proceedings:

A. Mahler and A. Lampen, "An Integrated Toolset for Engineering Software Configurations," *Proceedings of the ACM SIGSOFT/SIGPLAN Software Engineering*, Symposium on Practical Software Engineering Environments, Boston, Massachusetts, 28-30 November 1988. Reprinted in *SIGSOFT SE Notes*, vol. 13, no. 5, pp. 191-200, and *SIGPLAN NOTICES*, vol. 24, no. 2.

A. Lampen and A. Mahler, "An Object Base for Attributed Software Objects," *Proceedings of the EUUG Autumn '88 Conference*, Cascais, Portugal, 3-7 October 1988, pp. 95-105, European UNIX User Group, London, 1988.

Parallel and Distributed Implementations

Many implementations of *make* reflect the general trend in computing toward distributing a single job over multiple processors or multiple nodes in a network. The current state of the art in parallelization and distributed processing, however, still involves many hardware and operating system dependencies. Currently, the only platform-independent parallel *make* is the GNU implementation from the Free Software Foundation. AT&T's *nmake* also runs in parallel, and the Open Software Foundation (OSF) is planning to include a parallel *make* in its operating system. We should spend some time looking at the concepts behind this extension because it is sure to become important in the near future.

The typical tasks performed by *make* are ideal for parallelization. Most builds require the compilation of many independent source files, followed by a link of all the resulting object files. So the great bulk of the work—compilation—subdivides naturally into asynchronous, concurrent processes. The processes can simply exit after compilation, leaving just one to perform the final link. When you ask *make* to build multiple executables, parallelism can extend upward to that level, too.

The hard part of parallelization is recognizing when you have to perform particular commands in sequence, because one depends on the outcome of another. This requires dependence analysis, which is precisely *make*'s strength. To extend *make* for parallelism, therefore, a designer can build on its existing operations, adding the features offered by the operating system for fast process startup, synchronization, and scheduling.

Startup can be as simple as forking a new process (which *make* does already), but modern system programmers have found many ways to reduce the overhead of that operation. For instance, *nmake* keeps a special coshell in the background for handling multiple commands. Many operating systems also provide fast versions of *fork*, and alternatives like multi-threaded processes. For distributed processing on multiple network nodes, *make* can use Remote Procedure Calls (RPC).

Synchronization can be accomplished through operating system features such as semaphores.

Scheduling refers to keeping track of the available processors or nodes and assigning commands to them in the most efficient manner. A parallel *make* can do this automatically, but some implementations also offer you options for controlling the number of commands that run in parallel at any one time. While the ideal load would be one command per processor, a parallel *make* can often run faster than a sequential *make* even on a single-processor system. This is because *make*'s activities require a lot of file I/O, and thus include a lot of idle CPU time. Interleaving the commands therefore produces a speed-up even when these commands must share the CPU.

C

Features That Differ Between Variants of make

Background
List of Differences
Tests You Can Run

We have indicated throughout this book that some of the features we describe are missing from some variants of *make*, or might behave somewhat differently from one variant to another. This appendix explains how the divergences occurred, lists the features that can differ, and shows some tests you can run quickly to find out what your variant does. We have automated these tests in a series of shell scripts, which you can obtain for free from O'Reilly & Associates. See the Preface for ways to do this.

It is very hard to determine the source of the *make* offered on any particular system. Since *make* is a self-contained utility, vendors can easily substitute one set of sources for another. Someone at your site might have installed a special variant, like the GNU *make* from Free Software Foundation. Furthermore, vendors can add or remove features as they choose. Suffix rules are particularly easy (and appropriate) to customize for the vendor's utilities and build environment, so suffix rules are not even considered in this appendix.

This book documents mainly the current System V *make*. Many other variants have added valuable enhancements, but they vary so much from system to system that they could not be covered here. Therefore, it is worth your while to read the documentation for your version of *make*.

Finally, try out the shell scripts and related tests in this appendix. A feature might be in your version of *make* even though it is undocumented.

Background

The original *make* at AT&T is the brainchild of S.I. Feldman. (He is associated with several other significant projects there, including a FORTRAN 77 compiler that was possibly the first in the industry, and a FORTRAN-to-C converter that is in heavy use today.) Most of the outside world encountered the program in an enhanced version called "an augmented version of *make*," which was released with System V Release 2 of the UNIX operating system. This version laid the basis for future enhancements in both System V and in the Berkeley Standard Distribution (BSD).

The historic schism between System V and BSD affected *make* just like every other aspect of UNIX systems. Many important features entered System V Release 3, but were not added to BSD. The BSD version evolved in its own way and introduced some useful features, although these are not discussed in this book. By now, most commercial vendors have obtained System V *make* or added its features, but you could still find differences on your system.

For brief descriptions of major *make* extensions, see Appendix B.

List of Differences

The following table lists the major features of *make* that are not supported in all variants.

Features of make	Availability
Macro string substitution: `${FILES:.c=.o}`	Supported on System V, but not BSD 4.3.
File and directory macros: `${<F}` and `${<D}`	Supported on System V, but not BSD 4.3.
Target name available as `$$@` on its own dependency line	Supported on both System V and BSD 4.3, but not on GNU *make* and some other variants.

Features of make	Availability
Parenthesis syntax for libraries on dependency lines: libc.a(stat.o)	Supported on System V, but not BSD 4.3. GNU *make* supports the syntax for modules, but not for entry points.
Single-suffix rules (such as .c to executable).	Supported on System V, but not BSD 4.3.
.sh suffix rules for shell scripts.	Supported on systems that allow single-suffix rules.
Default shell.	Some variants use Bourne shell by default, while others inherit the user's SHELL environment variable. Some variants force the use of Bourne shell no matter what you set SHELL to. Some variants force the use of Bourne shell on top-level makes (those you enter on the command line) while allowing you to change the shell for recursive makes.
MAKE and MAKEFLAGS macros.	MAKE is included on System V, but not BSD 4.3. MAKEFLAGS is spelled MFLAGS on BSD 4.3.
include statement.	Supported on System V, but not BSD 4.3.
VPATH macro for viewpath.	Available on most systems, both System V and BSD.
VPATH used to search for prerequisites with relative pathnames.	Supported on System V, but not BSD 4.3.
VPATH used to search for implicit prerequisites.	Supported on most systems that support VPATH.
VPATH used to search for include files, description files, and words within command lines.	Supported on some systems that support VPATH.

Tests You Can Run

In this section, we offer some simple shell scripts and description files that help you test your variant of *make* for the features listed in this appendix.

Macro String Substitution

Create a *makefile* containing

```
STRING = abc

echo:
    echo ${STRING:c=X}
```

Then enter the command,

```
$ make
```

If the string **abX** appears, your variant supports System V macro string substitution. If *make* echoes a null string or issues an error message, your variant does not support macro string substitution.

File and Directory Macros

Create a *makefile* containing

```
directory/file :
    echo $(@F)
    echo $(@D)
```

Then enter the command,

```
$ make
```

If the strings **directory** and **file** both appear, your variant supports the F and D syntax. If **file** appears twice, or if one or both strings fail to appear, your variant does not support the syntax.

Target Name as $$@ on Dependency Lines

All variants of *make* support the $@ macro, which can be found in virtually every suffix rule and description file entry. But $@ cannot be used on the dependency line, for complicated reasons having to do with the order in which *make* expands dependency lines. Basically, *make* evaluates macros before creating its list of prerequisites, but the `$@` macro turns into a null string because it is not defined until later.

Because it is often useful to refer to a target name on its own dependency line, System V *make* includes a special work-around to support it. You must specify the name as `$$@`, with two dollar signs. The first gets stripped off during macro expansion. The rest is changed to the target name during later processing.

To check for this feature, create a *makefile* containing:

```
targ : $$@_as_dep
    echo $@ depends on $?
targ_as_dep :
```

Then enter the command,

```
$ make
```

If *make* echoes

```
targ depends on targ_as_dep
```

your variant supports the $$@ method of referring to a target on its own dependency line. If you see an error message, your variant cannot handle that feature.

Parenthesis Syntax for Libraries

Enter the command

```
$ make /lib/libc.a\(printf.o\)
```

where the backslashes are required by the shell. If you see a message like

```
`printf.o' is up to date.
```

your variant supports the use of parentheses for library modules. If you see a syntax error, your variant does not support that syntax.

We are assuming that every *libc.a* has an object file named *printf.o*, and that you won't get into trouble for just asking about it. But you can test parentheses almost as easily by creating a *makefile* of your own:

```
library(object) :
    echo $%
```

and then entering

```
$ make
```

If the string **object** appears, your variant supports the use of parentheses for library modules. If you see a null string or an error message, your variant does not support the use of parentheses.

In order to test support for entry points, you must have an actual library. Taking the lazy way out again, run *nm* to find the entry points in *libc.a*:

```
$ nm /lib/libc.a

printf.o:
0x00000000 U  ___iob
0x00000000 U  __doprnt
0x00000000 T  __printf
        .
        .
        .
```

Pick out one—perhaps *_printf*—and enter

```
$ make /lib/libc.a\(\(_printf\)\)
```

If your variant supports entry points, you will again get a message like:

```
`printf.o´ is up to date.
```

Single-suffix Rules and .sh Rules

Create a *makefile* containing:

```
.o :
      echo 'Prerequisite $< makes target $@'
```

Then enter the commands,

```
$ touch dummy.o
$ make dummy
```

If *make* echoes

```
Prerequisite dummy.o makes target dummy
```

your variant supports single-suffix rules. If you see an error message, your variant does not support such rules. You can check for **.sh** rules through the **–p** option described in Chapter 3, *Suffix Rules*.

Default Shell

Before trying all this stuff, consider that the experts recommend use of the Bourne shell in *make*. The safest course is to put `SHELL=/bin/sh` at the top of every description file, and skip the options in this section.

If you are still interested in testing your variant of *make*, start with the following *makefile*.

```
echo :
     echo ${SHELL}
```

Then, if you are in the Bourne shell, change your SHELL environment variable. You can set it to any string you like, such as:

```
$ SHELL=junk ; export SHELL
```

Then enter the command,

```
$ make
```

If *make* echoes the string to which you set SHELL, your variant allows the environment to determine the shell. (The */bin/echo* command should be able to run even if make cannot use a shell.) If *make* echoes `/bin/sh`, it enforces the use of the Bourne shell. In the latter case—after you reset your SHELL to the right pathname—you may want a more comprehensive test, as shown below.

Create the following *makefile*:

```
echo :
     echo ${SHELL}

recurs :
     make cshell SHELL=/bin/csh

cshell :
     echo ${SHELL}
     if ( -f makefile ) then ; echo cshell ; endif
```

Now enter

```
$ make cshell SHELL=/bin/csh
```

If *make* echoes `cshell` and exits normally, you can set the shell explicitly through a SHELL macro. If *make* encounters an error, it enforces the use of the Bourne shell at least at the top level. In the latter case, try entering

```
$ make recurs
```

A successful execution means that you can set the shell for recursive makes, while an error indicates that the Bourne shell is always used.

MAKE and MAKEFLAGS Macros

Print out the list of *make* defaults through the **–p** option, and see whether these are defined. You can use the following commands when interacting with the Bourne or Korn shell:

```
$ make -p 2>/dev/null| grep MAKE
MAKE = make
MAKEFLAGS = b
$ make -p 2>/dev/null| grep MFLAGS
$
```

The equivalent commands suppressing error messages in the C shell are:

```
% make -p |& grep MAKE
MAKE = make
MAKEFLAGS = b
% make -p |& grep MFLAGS
%
```

include Statement

The test in this section isn't elegant, but it's fast. Create a *makefile* containing

```
include dummymake

run :
     echo 'Running'
```

Then enter the commands,

```
$ echo 'DUMMY=' > dummymake
$ make
```

If *make* echoes `Running` and exits without an error message, your variant supports the `include` statement. If you get a syntax error message referring to line 1 of the description file, your variant does not support the statement.

VPATH

Create a *makefile* containing

```
check : file
     cp $? $@
     cp $? final_file

lowercheck : lower/file
     cat $?
```

Then enter the commands

```
$ mkdir sub
$ echo 'A file in the subdirectory' > sub/file
$ make check VPATH=sub
```

If *make* copies the *sub* file and exits normally, your variant supports VPATH; if you get an error message you have no support for VPATH. In the first case, you can check related features. Enter

```
$ mkdir sub/lower
$ echo 'A file in the lower subdirectory' > sub/lower/file
$ make lowercheck VPATH=sub
```

Successful execution means that your variant uses VPATH to search for relative pathnames; an error means it does not. Now check how far-reaching the use of VPATH is. Copy some source file to the *sub* directory—let's say you call it *dummy.c*—and enter

```
$ make dummy.o VPATH=sub
```

Successful execution means that your variant uses VPATH to search for implicit prerequisites; an error means it does not.

You can easily devise tests to check for other things that *make* can use VPATH to search for (include files, description files, words within command lines), but we strongly recommend that you do it just for your amusement. For real work, use VPATH only to find prerequisites.

Index

:, (see colon; double colon)
#, (see comment; pound sign)
$$, (see dollar sign; macro; shell
    variables)
%, (see percent sign)
( ), (see parentheses)
*, (see asterisk; metacharacter; pat-
    tern-matching)
., (see period)
;, (see semicolon)
<, (see less-than sign; metacharac-
    ter)
=, (see equal sign)
?, (see question mark; metacharac-
    ter; pattern-matching)
@, (see at-sign)
[ ], (see brackets)
`, (see backquote)
−, (see hyphen)
\, (see backslash)
_, (see underline)

{ }, (see braces)
˜, (see tilde)

A

.a suffix, (see library)
ar(1) command, defined, 33
    in default suffix rules, 35
    minimizing rebuilds, 35, 54
archive, (see ar(1) command;
    library)
AS macro, 41
ASFLAGS macro, 41
assembly language, (see source
    files; .s suffix)
asterisk (*), 57
    internal macro, 36, 112
at-sign (@), 95
    internal macro, 19, 36, 112

at-sign (@) (cont'd)
AT&T, history of System V
    make(1), 128
    nmake and mk, 116
    toolkit, 118

B

-b option, 97, 109
backquote (` `), storing results of
    command in a macro, 72
backslash (\), to continue line in
    description file, 7
    to continue long shell com-
    mand, 59, 105
backward chaining, 4, 117, 119
    limitations of, 48
bad octal character, error mes-
    sage, 101
Bell Labs, (see AT&T)
Berkeley Standard Distribution,
    version of make(1), 128,
    128-135
blank lines, in description files, 7
Bourne shell, 64
braces ({ }), in macro definitions,
    11
    optional use with single-charac-
    ter macros, 11, 21
brackets ([ ]), shell pattern-match-
    ing, 57
    test command in Bourne and
    Korn shells, 105
Brunhoff, Todd, 121-122
BSD, version of make(1), 128,
    128-135
    version of SCCS, 29
built-in commands, 60
    setenv, 14
    (see also environment vari-
    ables.)

C

.c suffix, 23
.c˜ suffix, handling by SCCS, 32
.c suffix, in relation to lex (.l) and
    yacc (.y) files, 38
C compiler, -c option, 39
    -D option, 26, 74, 78-85
    -D option CFLAGS macro; (see
    also CFLAGS macro; version
    control.)
    -g option, 26
    -l option, 26
    -M option, 86
    maintaining consistency across
    builds, 78-85
    -O option, 42
    -p option, 85
    suffix rules, 25
    using a non-standard version,
    12
C language source files, 23
C preprocessor, conditional com-
    pilation and version control,
    78
    used by Fortran .F files, 28
    used by imake, 121
    used by makedepend, 122
    used to find dependencies on
    header (include) files, 88
C shell, adding environment vari-
    ables, 14
cat(1) command, 7
CC macro, 41
cc(1) command, (see C compiler)
CFLAGS macro, 41
    adding to existing options, 74
    and -M compiler option, 87
    basic use for compiler options,
    26
    conditional compilation
    (#ifdef), 78-85
    default, 42
    maintaining consistency
    through recursive make, 79
    specifying multiple options, 26,
    74
chaining, limitations of, 48

method for tracing dependencies, 4, 117, 119
character, (see bad octal character; metacharacter; pattern-matching; individual characters)
clean, conventional target, 8, 80
clobber, conventional target, 69
colon (:), 3
  double (::), 37, 106
  inconsistent use of, 106
command, rcp(1), 90
  associated with target, 57-58
  built-in, 60
  cc(1) (see C compiler)
  echoing to standard output, 94
  linking, 3, 22, 26
  make(1) (see make(1) command)
  multi-line, 59, 105
  on dependency line, 7
  overriding suffix rules, 48
  setenv, 14
  status, 61-63
  storing in file from make(1) build, 94
  using output within a build, 72
command options, maintaining consistency, 27, 79, 82, 117, 124
  suffix rules, 26
comment, 7
compilation of makefile, 117
compiler, C, 86
  conventions, 53-54
  Fortran, 28
  Pascal, 29
  suffix rules, 25, 43-46
  using a non-standard version, 12
  which language used by suffix rules, 24, 47
conditional macro definition, 79
conventions, compiling, 53-54
  naming, 53-54
coshell, 117

cpp(1) command, see C preprocessor, 28
csh, (see C shell)
.cshrc file, (see environment variables)
current target name (in command lines ($@)), 19
current target name (in dependency lines ($$@)), 20

D

-d option, 99-100, 109
.DEFAULT target, 97
D modifier for macros, 74
date, (see dependency relations; modification time)
debug option (-d), 99-100
debugging, 94-95
definition, macro, 9, 12
  macro and #ifdef, 78-85
  suffix rules, 49-50
dependency line, 3
  command on, 7
  inconsistent use of double colon, 106
  order in relation to macros, 12, 89
  problems with, 106
  semicolon to start command, 7
  with double colon, 37
dependency relations, among files, 1-2
  non-existent file, 8, 80
  testing, 95
dependent, 1
  (see also prerequisite.)
description file, 2
  compatibility with earlier implementations, 97
  conventional .mk suffix, 94
  making maintenance easier, 10
  rules and format, 7
diff(1) command, exit status, 60
directory, alternate for SCCS, 31
  as macro, 10, 66

directory (cont'd)
  handling in make(1), 70, 74-75
  using viewpath (VPATH macro),
    75
distributed file system, problems
  with make(1), 90
distributed files, problems with
  make(1), 89
distributed processing, and
  make(1), 125
dollar sign, as macro, 41
  in macro, 9
  in shell variables, 61
doname, in output from -d option,
  100
  in recursive make, 100
double colon (::), 37
double parentheses (( )), 35
Dubois, Paul, 122
dummy target, 68
  dependencies in relation to
    actual files, 80
  using suffix rules, 54

E

−e option, 15, 109
.e suffix, 28
.e˜ suffix, handling by SCCS, 32
EFL, source files, 28
entry point, module within library,
  33, 35
  name, 33, 35
envflg, in output from -d option,
  100
environment, for software development, 65-66
environment variables, adding,
  14
  in .profile/.cshrc/.login file, 14
  MAKEFLAGS and MFLAGS, 97
  printing out, 40
  priority of, 14
  relation to macros, 13-18
  to control directories on large
    projects, 66
  weakness of, 17

eqn, example of suffix rules to
  support document production,
    50
equal sign (=), defining variables
  in Bourne shell, 13-14
  in macro definition, 10, 111
  on make(1) command line, 13,
    109
error, 96
  $! nulled, predecessor cycle,
    106
  bad octal character, 101
  branching on exit status from
    command in description file,
      62
  cannot load command, 103
  command not found, 103
  couldn't load shell, 104
  don't know how to make, 101
  from command in description
    file, 61-63
  ignoring exit status from com-
    mand in description file, 62
  inconsistent rules lines, 106
  infinitely recursive macro?, 107
  messages, 99-108
  must be a separator, 101
  syntax, 101, 105
  syntax error in description file,
    101
  target up-to-date, 102
  too many command lines, 106
error codes, ignoring, 96
executable files, building large
  numbers of, 21
exit, branching on status from
  command in description file,
    62
  from make(1), 60
  status from command in
    description file, 61-63
  status from make(1) command,
    95
exit command, in description files,
  60
extensions to make(1), 116-126
  GNU make, 118-119, 128-129
  imake, 119

extensions to make(1) (cont'd)
  makedepend, 122
  mk, 116
  nmake, 116
  shape, 123

F

–f option, 40, 94, 110
  in recursive make, 73
.F suffix, 28
.f suffix, 28
.f˜ suffix, handling by SCCS, 32
F modifier for macros, 74
f77(1) command, 28
  (see also Fortran.)
FC macro, 41
fc(1) command, 28
  (see also Fortran.)
Feldman, S. I., 128
FFLAGS macro, 41
file, (see dependency relations;
    description file; directory;
    object file; pathname; prereq-
    uisite; source file; suffixes;
    target)
flag, (see FLAGS macros; option)
FLAGS macros, in suffix rules, 26,
  43-46
forcing rebuilds, 80-82, 86
fork, running commands in
    make(1), 64, 117, 126
formatting macros (nroff/troff),
  50
Fortran, source files, 28
Fowler, Glenn, 118
FRC macro and target, 80-82, 86
Free Software Foundation,
  118-119
Fulton, Jim, 121
function, module within library, 35
future of make(1), 125

G

GET macro, 41
get(1) command (SCCS), 31
GFLAGS macro, 31, 41
GNU make, 100, 118-119, 125,
  128-129
grep(1) command, exit status, 60

H

.h files, dependencies, 67, 85-88
  listing on separate dependency
    lines, 8
.h˜ suffix, handling by SCCS, 32
.h suffix, suffix rule for, 43
.h files, dependencies, 117, 122
header files, dependencies, 67,
  85-88, 117, 122
hidden dependencies, 67, 117,
  122
Hume, Andrew, 116
hyphen (–), as name of description
    file, 40, 94, 110
  to ignore errors, 62

I

–i option, 62, 96, 110
#ifdef, use with macros, 78-85
.IGNORE target, 62, 96
imake, 119, 122
include files, dependencies, 67,
  85-88, 117, 122
**include statement (including
    description files)**, 88-89
install, conventional target, 69
internal macro, $@, 19
  19-22
  $$@, 20
  $?, 20
  $<, 25
  $*, 27, 31
  $<, 31
  $%, 36
  $*, 36

internal macro (cont'd)
  $<, 36
  $@, 36
  $$@, 112
  $%, 112
  $*, 112
  $<, 112
  $?, 112
  $@, 112
  in suffix rules, 27

K

–k option, 62, 110
Koch, Wilfried, 125

L

–l linker option, as macro, 26
.l suffix, 38
.l˜ suffix, handling by SCCS, 32
Lampen, Andreas, 125
last-modified time, and NFS, 90
  defined, 3
  in output of -d (debug) option,
    100
LD macro, 41
ld(1) command, (see linker command)
LDFLAGS macro, 41
less-than sign (<), internal macro,
    25, 36, 112
LEX macro, 41
lex(1) command, 38
  dependency on yacc file, 38
lex.yy.c file, 38
LFLAGS macro, 41
library, and -l linker option, 26
  as prerequisite, 34, 36-37
  as target, 33, 37
  maintaining under make(1),
    33-38
  of object modules, 35
  on viewpath (VPATH macro), 77
  structure of, 33

  updating all modules in single
    command, 54
linker command, 3
  -l option, 26
  macros in command line, 22
.login file, (see environment variables)
lp(1) command, 52
lpr(1) command, 52

M

.mk suffix, 94
macro, 74
  changing definitions during a
    build, 12, 72, 79
  D modifier, 74, 112
  defined, 9
  F modifier, 74, 112
  formatting (nroff/troff), 50
  internal, 19-22, 74
  MAKEFLAGS, 96
  modifier (D and F), 74, 112
  order in relation to dependency
    lines, 12, 89
  string substitution, 18
  undefined, 11
macro definitions, 9, 12
  allowing user-specified
    defaults, 16
  and #ifdef symbols, 78-85
  conditional, 79
  current, 39-46
  default, 39-46
  including macros in, 11
  null string, 11
  overriding priority, 15
  printing, 39-46
  printing out, 40
  priority of, 14
  string substitution, 18
  suffix substitution, 18
Mahler, Axel, 125
maintaining description files,
    allowing for changes in directories, 10, 66, 76
  macros, 10

maintaining description files (cont'd)
multiple description files for different directories, 71
preventing unnecessary builds, 95
storing under SCCS, 32
MAKE macro, 41
make(1) command, exit status, 95
exiting from, 60, 96
options, 93, 109-110
recursive invocation of, 70
requirements for invoking, 5-6
suppressing execution, 40, 94
with no target, 6
make(1) concept, extensions, 116-126
future of, 125
history, 128
limitations of, 67, 115
models for understanding, ix, xi-1, 4
parallelism, 125
strengths of, 3-5
theory behind, 3
make(1) variants, $$@ for target on dependency lines, 20, 130
Berkeley Standard Distribution (BSD), 128, 128-135
conditional macro definition, 79, 118
differences in MAKEFLAGS and MFLAGS, 97
entry points in library names, 35, 132
F and D modifiers to macros, 74, 130
finding SCCS files in *SCCS* directory, 31
GNU, 100, 118-119, 128-129
include statement, 88, 134
macro string substitution, 18, 130
major differences between, 128-129
MAKE macro, 73, 134
MAKEFLAGS and MFLAGS macros, 96, 134

modules in library names, 35, 131
reasons for differences, 127
.sh suffix, 32
shell used to execute commands, 64, 133
single-suffix rules, 39, 132
state file, 82, 117
Sun Microsystems, 86, 100
System V, 127-135
testing for, 128-135
use of parentheses in library names, 35, 131
viewpaths (VPATH macro), 75, 134
makedepend, 122
used in imake, 121
makefile, (see description file)
makefile.ms, nmake state file, 117
makefile.so, nmake compiled description file, 117
MAKEFLAGS macro, 41, 96
markfile target, 42
McGrath, Roland, 119
messages, 99-108
$! nulled, predecessor cycle, 106
bad octal character, 101
cannot load command, 103
command not found, 103
couldn't load shell, 104
don't know how to make, 101
inconsistent rules lines, 106
infinitely recursive macro?, 107
must be a separator, 101
syntax error, 101, 105
syntax error in description file, 101
target up-to-date, 102
too many command lines, 106
metacharacter, effect in make(1) execution of commands, 64
interpreted by make(1), 57
permitted in commands, 57
MFLAGS macro, (see MAKEFLAGS macro)
MIT Project Athena, 121-122
mk, 116

.mk suffix, 94
modification time, and NFS, 90
 defined, 3
 in output of -d (debug) option,
  100
module, 23
 library of, 54
 structure of library, 33
 within library, 35
Moraes, Mark, 122
multi-line shell commands, 59,
 105
mv(1) command, robustness of -f
 option, 62

N

−n option, 40, 94, 110
naming conventions, suffixes
 used by compilers, 23, 53
 writing your own suffix rules,
  48
network, distributed processing,
 125
 problems with make(1), 89
new suffixes, 51
newline, in commands, 59-60
 in macro definition, 11
 overriding, 59
NFS, problems with make(1), 90
nm(1) command, to find module
 (entry point) name, 35
nmake, 116
noreset, in output from -d option,
 100
nroff, preprocessors, 50
 sample description file, 49-54
 support for in nmake, 117
null string, for undefined macro,
 11
 in macro definition, 11
null suffix, 39

O

.o suffix, 23
object file, possible prerequisites,
 28, 47
 structure of library, 33
 within library, 35
object module, 23
 library of, 35, 54
 structure of library, 33
 within library, 35
Obst, Wolfgang, 125
Open Software Foundation, 125
options, as FLAGS macros in suffix
 rules, 26
options to cc(1) command, -l, 26
options to ld(1) command, -l, 26
options to make(1) command, −
 (hyphen), 40, 94, 110
 -b, 97, 109
 -d, 99-100, 109
 -e, 15, 109
 -f, 40, 110
 -i, 62, 96, 110
 -k, 62, 110
 -n, 40, 94, 110
 -p, 40, 110
 -q, 95, 110
 -r, 97, 110
 -s, 40, 95, 110
 -t, 95, 110
OSF, 125
out-of-date, 3
 (see also dependency relations;
  modification time.)

P

−p option, 40, 110
 in recursive make, 41
.p suffix, as convention for profiled
 object files, 85
 for Pascal files, 29
parallel make(1), 117-118, 125
parentheses ( ), doubled in specifying a library, 35
 in macro definitions, 11

parentheses ( ) (cont'd)
  in shell command, 37
  in specifying a library, 35, 54
  optional use with single-charac-
    ter macros, 11, 21
Pascal, source files, 29
path, (see directory; pathname;
    VPATH)
pathname, dividing into directory
    and file portions, 74
  handling in make(1), 70, 74
  specifying full, 65
  viewpath (VPATH macro),
    75-80
pattern-matching, percent sign
    (%) extension, 19, 116
  percent-sign (%) extension, 118
pattern-matching characters, 57
  permitted in commands, 57
pc(1) command, 29
percent sign (%), for pattern-
    matching, 19, 116, 118
  internal macro, 36, 112
period, in suffix rules, 24, 50-51,
    111
  in .SUFFIXES line, 51, 113
  matched by make(1) wildcard
    in files, 58
pic, example of suffix rules to sup-
    port document production, 50
pound sign (#), to start comment
    in description file, 7
Pralle, Ulrich, 125
.PRECIOUS target, 96
preprocessor, (see C preproces-
    sor; EFL; Ratfor; troff)
prerequisite, defined, 1
  in $? macro, 20
  in $< macro, 25
  in $% macro, 36
  in $* macro, 36
  in $< macro, 36
  more recently modified, 20
  with double colon (::), 37
print option (-p), 40
process, in parallel make(1), 126

  multithreaded in parallel
    make(1), 126
  number as shell variable, 61
  scheduling, 64, 117, 126
  use of coshell in nmake, 117
.profile file, (see environment vari-
    ables)
Project Athena, 121-122
Prolog, model for make(1), 4
punctuation, (see metacharacter;
    also individual characters)

Q

−q option, 95, 110
question mark (?), 57
  internal macro, 20, 112
question option (-q), 95

R

−r option, 97, 110
.r suffix, 28
.r˜ suffix, handling by SCCS, 32
Ratfor, source files, 28
RCS (Revision Control System),
    32
  and GNU make, 119
rcp(1) command, 90
recursive invocation of make(1),
    70
redefining, suffix rules, 48
remote copy command, 90
remote procedure call, in parallel
    make(1), 126
remote processing, parallel
    make(1), 126
  problems with make(1), 89
removing files, automatically done
    in suffix rules, 43
  keeping when make(1) fails, 96
  make clean, 8, 80
  make clobber, 69
rm(1) command, robustness of -f
    option, 62
RPC, in parallel make(1), 126

rules, (see dependency line; suffix rules)
rules line, 3, 101, 106
(see also dependency line.)

S

–s option, 40, 95, 110
.s suffix, 23
.s˜ suffix, handling by SCCS, 32
.SUFFIXES target, 24, 49
s. prefix (SCCS), 29
SCCS, 29, 32
automatic retrieval of files, 29
directory, 31
scheduling processes, in make(1), 64
in nmake, 117
in parallel make(1), 126
script, (see shell script)
security and pathnames, 65
semicolon (;), on dependency line, 7, 110
to nullify a suffix rule, 55
to separate parts of a command, 60, 105
setenv command, 14
(see also environment variables.)
sh, (see shell; SHELL macro; shell script)
.sh suffix, 32
.sh˜ suffix, handling by SCCS, 32
shape, 123
shell, Bourne, 64
C, 14, 64
strengths contrasted with make(1), 58
when used to run a command in make(1), 64
shell commands, built-in, 60
multi-line, 59, 105
SHELL macro, recommended setting, 64
testing how handled in make(1), 133

shell programming, (see shell script)
shell script, as wrapper for make(1), 17
incorporating into description file, 59-62, 105, 117
invoking within description file, 57
maintained through SCCS and make, 32
strengths contrasted with make(1), 58
shell variables, 40, 61
$$ for process number, 61
adding to environment, 14, 16
defining, 14
in .profile/.cshrc/.login file, 14
MAKEFLAGS and MFLAGS, 97
priority of, 14
process number, 61
relation to macros, 13-18
significant suffixes, 24
single suffix, in suffix rules, 39
s.makefile, 32
software development, environment for, 65-66
source code control system, (see SCCS)
source files, assembly language, 23
assembly language .s suffix; (see also .s suffix.)
C language, 23
Fortran, 28
lex, 38
on viewpath (VPATH macro), 77
Pascal, 29
yacc, 38
space, after backslash, 7, 11, 105, 110-111
in command within description file, 111
in dependency line, 110
in include statement, 111
in macro definitions, 11, 111
in suffix rule dependency line, 111
in suffix rules, 51

space (cont'd)
  in .SUFFIXES line, 113
special targets, 93, 113
spell(1) command, 59
standard input, as description file,
    110
state file, 82, 117
status, branching on exit status
      from command in description
      file, 62
    from command in description
      file, 61-63
    from make(1) command, 95
    ignoring exit status from com-
      mand in description file, 62
status information, 94-95
string substitution, 18
suffix, single, 39
suffix rules, adding new suffixes,
    51
    command options, 26
    compared to macros and string
      substitution, 19
    conflicting meanings for suf-
      fixes, 51, 56
    current, 39-46
    default, 39-46
    defining, 49-50
    for SCCS files, 29, 32
    how they work, 24-25, 27
    internal macros in, 27
    order of, 54
    overridden by commands in
      description file, 48
    overriding, 54-55
    precedence, 46-48
    printing, 39-46
    redefining, 48
    spaces in, 51
    to distinguish versions of files,
      85
    to support targets that are not
      files, 54
    types of, 28
    using single suffix, 39
    writing your own, 48-50
suffixes, .c, 23
    conflicting meanings, 51, 56
    current, 39-46
    default, 39-46
    .e, 28
    .F, 28
    .f, 28
    .mk, 94
    new, 49, 51
    null, 39
    .o, 23
    order of, 51, 54
    .p, 29
    precedence, 46-48
    printing, 39
    .r, 28
    .s, 23
    significant, 24, 49
    to distinguish versions of files,
      85
.SUFFIXES target, 24, 49
Sun Microsystems, make(1), 86,
    100
    NFS, 90
symbol, (see #ifdef, macro)
System V make(1), as basis for
    this book, xi
    history of, 128

                    T

−t option, 95, 110
tab, in command within descrip-
    tion file, 7, 111
    initial, 3
target, continuing to build targets
      despite errors, 62
    current, 39-46
    current (in command lines
      ($@)), 19
    current (in dependency lines
      ($$@)), 20
    default, 6
    .DEFAULT, 97
    default, 97
    defined, 1
    dependency relations of non-
      existent file, 8, 80
    .IGNORE, 62, 96

target (cont'd)
  markfile, 42
  multiple on one dependency
    line, 20
  .PRECIOUS, 96
  printing entries, 39-46
  special, 93
  .SUFFIXES, 49
  that is not a filename, 8, 68
  with double colon (::), 37
tbl, example of suffix rules to support document production, 50
Technical University of Berlin,
  125
Tektronix, 121-122
threads, in parallel make(1), 126
tilde (⁀), problems in shell commands, 64
  SCCS file in suffix rules, 30
TIME, in output from -d option,
  100
timestamp, (see dependency relations; modification time)
touch, -t option, 95
  to record that an operation was
    performed, 70
troff, preprocessors, 50
  sample description file, 49-54
  support for in nmake, 117
troubleshooting, 99-108
true(1) command, to nullify a suffix rule, 55

U

underline (_), in macro name, 11
usage, make(1) command line, 93,
  109-110

V

variable, 97
  environment, 13-18, 14
  printing out shell, 40
  process number, 61
  shell, 13-18

  (see also macro, MAKEFLAGS
    and MFLAGS in shell environ-
    ment.)
variant, (see RCS; SCCS; version
  control; C compiler; make(1)
  variants)
version, SCCS source control, 29
  (see RCS; SCCS)
version control, building libraries
  from object files compiled
  with different options, 37
  conditional compilation
    (#ifdef), 78
  files shared by several program-
    mers, 68
  imake extension, 120
  programs that share source files,
    4
  RCS, 32
  SCCS, 29-32
  shape extension, 123
  through viewpath (VPATH
    macro), 76
viewpath, (see VPATH)
VPATH macro, 75-80
  to find files in SCCS directory,
    31

W

what(1) command, 42
white space, (see space; tab; newline)
**wildcard pattern-matching char-
  acters,** interpreted by
  make(1), 57
  permitted in commands, 57
wrapper shell script, to set up
  environment for make(1), 17

X

X Consortium, 121-122
X Window System, 119

Y

.y suffix, 38
.y˜ suffix, handling by SCCS, 32
YACC macro, 41
yacc(1) command, 38
  -d option, 38
YFLAGS, to hold -d option, 38
YFLAGS macro, 41
y.tab.c file, 38
y.tab.h file, 38

About the Authors

Over a ten-year career in computer documentation, Andrew Oram has evolved from a proponent of the congenial user-oriented approach to a fanatic on the subject of explaining models and internal operations so as to empower computer users. He was not prepared by education (which includes music and social work) for the philosophical and pedagogical demands of this role, but seems to have fallen into it.

His technical writing career includes Honeywell Information Systems (now Bull), CSPI (still itself, incredibly), MASSCOMP (now Concurrent Computer Corporation), and Hitachi Computer Products. He has also taught PDP-11 assembly language. Topics of his manuals include network administration and programming, array processors, languages, debuggers, and real-time programming—in fact, writing about shell commands in *Managing Projects with make* has proven to be a relaxing break.

Currently he works for O'Reilly & Associates as an editor, and pursues research in creating documentation around the design of software and computer systems.

With a background in journalism and farming, Steve Talbott has worked for the past 10 years in technical documentation. Prior to joining O'Reilly Associates he managed the Technical Publications Group at Concurrent Computer Corporation, and before that was responsible for the development of computer-based documentation tools at Concurrent. In his current editorial position at O'Reilly, he helps to develop new titles across the company's product line. Avocationally, Steve pursues an interest in the broader social and cultural implications of computers.

Colophon

Our look is the result of reader comments, our own experimentation, and distribution channels.

Distinctive covers complement our distinctive approach to UNIX documentation, breathing personality and life into potentially dry subjects. UNIX and its attendant programs can be unruly beasts. Nutshell Handbooks help you tame them.

The animal featured on the cover of *Managing Projects with make* is a potto, a member of the loris family. A small primate native to the tropical forests of West Africa, the potto is 17 inches long and covered with dense, wooly, reddish-brown fur. Its opposable thumbs give it an excellent grasp, leaving it well adapted to its life in the trees. The potto spends its days sleeping in crevices or holes in trees, emerging at night to hunt for food—insects, snails, bats and fruit. Unlike many primates, the potto generally lives alone.

Edie Freedman designed this cover and the entire UNIX bestiary that appears on other Nutshell Handbooks. The beasts themselves are adapted from 19th-century engravings from the Dover Pictorial Archive.

The text of this book is set in Times Roman; headings are Helvetica; examples are Courier. Text was prepared using SoftQuad's *sqtroff* text formatter. Figures are produced with a Macintosh. Printing is done on an Apple LaserWriter.

More Titles from O'Reilly

UNIX Tools

The UNIX CD Bookshelf, 2nd Edition

By O'Reilly & Associates, Inc.
2nd Edition February 2000
624 pages, Features CD-ROM
ISBN 0-596-00000-6

The second edition of *The UNIX CD Bookshelf* contains six books from O'Reilly, plus the software from *UNIX Power Tools* – all on a convenient CD-ROM. Buyers also get a bonus hard-copy book, *UNIX in a Nutshell*, 3rd Edition. The CD-ROM contains *UNIX in a Nutshell, 3rd Edition; UNIX Power Tools, 2nd Edition* (with software); *Learning the UNIX Operating System, 4th Edition; Learning the vi Editor, 6th Edition; sed & awk, 2nd Edition;* and *Learning the Korn Shell*.

sed & awk, 2nd Edition

By Dale Dougherty & Arnold Robbins
2nd Edition March 1997
432 pages, ISBN 1-56592-225-5

sed & awk describes two text manipulation programs that are mainstays of the UNIX programmer's toolbox. This edition covers the sed and awk programs as they are mandated by the POSIX standard and includes discussion of the GNU versions of these programs.

lex & yacc, 2nd Edition

By John Levine, Tony Mason & Doug Brown
2nd Edition October 1992
366 pages, ISBN 1-56592-000-7

Shows programmers how to use two UNIX utilities, lex and yacc, in program development. You'll find tutorial sections for novice users, reference sections for advanced users, and a detailed index. Major MS-DOS and UNIX versions of lex and yacc are explored in depth. Also covers Bison and Flex.

sed & awk Pocket Reference

By Arnold Robbins
1st Edition January 2000
50 pages, ISBN 1-56592-729-X

The *sed & awk Pocket Reference* is a companion volume to *sed & awk*, 2nd Edition, and *Unix in a Nutshell*, 3rd Edition. This small book is a handy reference guide to the information presented in the larger volumes, presenting a concise summary of regular expressions and pattern matching, and summaries of sed and awk.

Writing GNU Emacs Extensions

By Bob Glickstein
1st Edition April 1997
236 pages, ISBN 1-56592-261-1

This book introduces Emacs Lisp and tells you how to make the editor do whatever you want, whether it's altering the way text scrolls or inventing a whole new "major mode." Topics progress from simple to complex, from lists, symbols, and keyboard commands to syntax tables, macro templates, and error recovery.

UNIX Power Tools, 2nd Edition

By Jerry Peek, Tim O'Reilly & Mike Loukides
2nd Edition August 1997
1120 pages, Includes CD-ROM
ISBN 1-56592-260-3

Loaded with practical advice about almost every aspect of UNIX, this second edition of *UNIX Power Tools* addresses the technology that UNIX users face today. You'll find thorough coverage of POSIX utilities, including GNU versions, detailed bash and tcsh shell coverage, a strong emphasis on Perl, and a CD-ROM that contains the best freeware available.

UNIX Tools

Practical Internet Groupware

By Jon Udell
1st Edition October 1999
524 pages, ISBN 1-56592-537-8

This revolutionary book tells users, programmers, IS managers, and system administrators how to build Internet groupware applications that organize the casual and chaotic transmission of online information into useful, disciplined, and documented data.

Learning the bash Shell, 2nd Edition

By Cameron Newham & Bill Rosenblatt
2nd Edition January 1998
336 pages, ISBN 1-56592-347-2

This second edition covers all of the features of bash Version 2.0, while still applying to bash Version 1.x. It includes one-dimensional arrays, parameter expansion, more pattern-matching operations, new commands, security improvements, additions to ReadLine, improved configuration and installation, and an additional programming aid, the bash shell debugger.

Applying RCS and SCCS

By Don Bolinger & Tan Bronson
1st Edition September 1995
528 pages, ISBN 1-56592-117-8

Applying RCS and SCCS is a thorough introduction to these two systems, viewed as tools for project management. This book takes the reader from basic source control of a single file, through working with multiple releases of a software project, to coordinating multiple developers. It also presents TCCS, a representative "front-end" that addresses problems RCS and SCCS can't handle alone, such as managing groups of files, developing for multiple platforms, and linking public and private development areas.

Software Portability with imake, 2nd Edition

By Paul DuBois
2nd Edition September 1996
410 pages, ISBN 1-56592-226-3

This handbook is ideal for X and UNIX programmers who want their software to be portable. The second edition covers version X11R6.1 of the X Window System, using imake for non-UNIX systems such as Windows NT, and some of the quirks about using imake under OpenWindows/Solaris.

MySQL & mSQL

By Randy Jay Yarger,
George Reese & Tim King
1st Edition July 1999
506 pages, ISBN 1-56592-434-7

This book teaches you how to use MySQL and mSQL, two popular and robust database products that support key subsets of SQL on both Linux and UNIX systems. Anyone who knows basic C, Java, Perl, or Python can write a program to interact with a database, either as a stand-alone application or through a Web page. This book takes you through the whole process, from installation and configuration to programming interfaces and basic administration. Includes ample tutorial material.

Programming with GNU Software

By Mike Loukides & Andy Oram
1st Edition December 1996
260 pages, Includes CD-ROM
ISBN 1-56592-112-7

This book and CD combination is a complete package for programmers who are new to UNIX or who would like to make better use of the system. The tools come from Cygnus Support, Inc., and Cyclic Software, companies that provide support for free software. Contents include GNU Emacs, gcc, C and C++ libraries, gdb, RCS, and make. The book provides an introduction to all these tools for a C programmer.

UNIX Basics

Learning the UNIX Operating System, 4th Edition

By Jerry Peek, Grace Todino & John Strang
4th Edition December 1997
106 pages, ISBN 1-56592-390-1

If you are new to UNIX, this concise introduction will tell you just what you need to get started and no more. The new fourth edition covers the Linux operating system and is an ideal primer for someone just starting with UNIX or Linux, as well as for Mac and PC users who encounter a UNIX system on the Internet. This classic book, still the most effective introduction to UNIX in print, now includes a quick-reference card.

Learning the vi Editor, 6th Edition

By Linda Lamb & Arnold Robbins
6th Edition October 1998
348 pages, ISBN 1-56592-426-6

This completely updated guide to editing with vi, the editor available on nearly every UNIX system, now covers four popular vi clones and includes command summaries for easy reference. It starts with the basics, followed by more advanced editing tools, such as ex commands, global search and replacement, and a new feature, multi-screen editing.

Learning GNU Emacs, 2nd Edition

By Debra Cameron, Bill Rosenblatt & Eric Raymond
2nd Edition September 1996
560 pages, ISBN 1-56592-152-6

Learning GNU Emacs is an introduction to Version 19.30 of the GNU Emacs editor, one of the most widely used and powerful editors available under UNIX. It provides a solid introduction to basic editing, a look at several important "editing modes" (special Emacs features for editing specific types of documents, including email, Usenet News, and the World Wide Web), and a brief introduction to customization and Emacs LISP programming. The book is aimed at new Emacs users, whether or not they are programmers. Includes quick-reference card.

Learning the Korn Shell

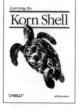

By Bill Rosenblatt
1st Edition June 1993
360 pages, ISBN 1-56592-054-6

A thorough introduction to the Korn shell, both as a user interface and as a programming language. This book provides a clear explanation of the Korn shell's features, including ksh string operations, co-processes, signals and signal handling, and command-line interpretation. Learning the Korn Shell also includes real-life programming examples and a Korn shell debugger (kshdb).

Using csh and tcsh

By Paul DuBois
1st Edition August 1995
242 pages, ISBN 1-56592-132-1

Using csh and tcsh describes from the beginning how to use these shells interactively to get your work done faster with less typing. You'll learn how to make your prompt tell you where you are (no more pwd); use what you've typed before (history); type long command lines with few keystrokes (command and filename completion); remind yourself of filenames when in the middle of typing a command; and edit a botched command without retyping it.

UNIX in a Nutshell: System V Edition, 3rd Edition

By Arnold Robbins
3rd Edition September 1999
616 pages, ISBN 1-56592-427-4

The bestselling, most informative UNIX reference book is now more complete and up-to-date. Not a scaled-down quick reference of common commands, UNIX in a Nutshell is a complete reference containing all commands and options, with descriptions and examples that put the commands in context. For all but the thorniest UNIX problems, this one reference should be all you need. Covers System V Release 4 and Solaris 7.

UNIX Basics

Learning the bash Shell, 2nd Edition

By Cameron Newham & Bill Rosenblatt
2nd Edition January 1998
336 pages, ISBN 1-56592-347-2

This second edition covers all of the features of bash Version 2.0, while still applying to bash Version 1.x. It includes one-dimensional arrays, parameter expansion, more pattern-matching operations, new commands, security improvements, additions to ReadLine, improved configuration and installation, and an additional programming aid, the bash shell debugger.

GNU Emacs Pocket Reference

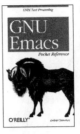

By Debra Cameron
1st Edition November 1998
64 pages, ISBN 1-56592-496-7

O'Reilly's *Learning GNU Emacs* covers the most popular and widespread of the Emacs family of editors. The *GNU Emacs Pocket Reference* is a companion volume to *Learning GNU Emacs*. This small book, covering Emacs version 20, is a handy reference guide to the basic elements of this powerful editor, presenting the Emacs commands in an easy-to-use tabular format.

UNIX Programming

POSIX Programmer's Guide

By Donald Lewine
1st Edition April 1991
640 pages, ISBN 0-937175-73-0

Most UNIX systems today are POSIX compliant because the federal government requires it for its purchases. Given the manufacturer's documentation, however, it can be difficult to distinguish system-specific features from those features defined by POSIX. The *POSIX Programmer's Guide*, intended as an explanation of the POSIX standard and as a reference for the POSIX.1 programming library, helps you write more portable programs.

Power Programming with RPC

By John Bloomer
1st Edition February 1992
522 pages, ISBN 0-937175-77-3

RPC (Remote Procedure Calling) is the ability to distribute the execution of functions on remote computers. Written from a programmer's perspective, this book shows what you can do with RPCs, like Sun RPC, the de facto standard on UNIX systems. It covers related programming topics for Sun and other UNIX systems and teaches through examples.

Pthreads Programming

By Bradford Nichols, Dick Buttlar & Jacqueline Proulx Farrell
1st Edition September 1996
284 pages, ISBN 1-56592-115-1

POSIX threads, or pthreads, allow multiple tasks to run concurrently within the same program. This book discusses when to use threads and how to make them efficient. It features realistic examples, a look behind the scenes at the implementation and performance issues, and special topics such as DCE and real-time extensions.

High Performance Computing, 2nd Edition

By Kevin Dowd & Charles Severance
2nd Edition July 1998
466 pages, ISBN 1-56592-312-X

This new edition of *High Performance Computing* gives a thorough overview of the latest workstation and PC architectures and the trends that will influence the next generation. It pays special attention to memory design, tuning code for the best performance, multiprocessors, and benchmarking.

O'REILLY®

UNIX Programming

POSIX.4

By Bill O. Gallmeister
1st Edition January 1995
568 pages, ISBN 1-56592-074-0

A general introduction to real-time programming and real-time issues, this book covers the POSIX.4 standard and how to use it to solve "real-world" problems. If you're at all interested in real-time applications – which include just about everything from telemetry to transaction processing – this book is for you. An essential reference.

CVS Pocket Reference

By Gregor N. Purdy
1st Edition August 2000
79 pages, ISBN 0-596-00003-0

The *CVS Pocket Reference* is a quick reference guide to help administrators and users set up and manage source code development. This small book, the ultimate companion for open source developers, covers CVS Version 1.10.8 and delivers the core concepts of version control, along with a complete command reference and guide to configuration and repository setup.

UNIX Systems Programming for SVR4

By David A. Curry
1st Edition July 1996
620 pages, ISBN 1-56592-163-1

Presents a comprehensive look at the nitty gritty details on how UNIX interacts with applications. If you're writing an application from scratch, or if you're porting an application to any System V.4 platform, you need this book. It thoroughly explains all UNIX system calls and library routines related to systems programming, working with I/O, files and directories, processing multiple input streams, file and record locking, and memory-mapped files.

O'REILLY®

TO ORDER: **800-998-9938** • **order@oreilly.com** • **http://www.oreilly.com/**
OUR PRODUCTS ARE AVAILABLE AT A BOOKSTORE OR SOFTWARE STORE NEAR YOU.
FOR INFORMATION: **800-998-9938** • **707-829-0515** • **info@oreilly.com**

How to stay in touch with O'Reilly

1. Visit Our Award-Winning Site

http://www.oreilly.com/

★ "Top 100 Sites on the Web" —*PC Magazine*
★ "Top 5% Web sites" —*Point Communications*
★ "3-Star site" —*The McKinley Group*

Our web site contains a library of comprehensive product information (including book excerpts and tables of contents), downloadable software, background articles, interviews with technology leaders, links to relevant sites, book cover art, and more. File us in your Bookmarks or Hotlist!

2. Join Our Email Mailing Lists

New Product Releases
To receive automatic email with brief descriptions of all new O'Reilly products as they are released, send email to:
ora-news-subscribe@lists.oreilly.com
Put the following information in the first line of your message (*not* in the Subject field):
subscribe ora-news

O'Reilly Events
If you'd also like us to send information about trade show events, special promotions, and other O'Reilly events, send email to:
ora-news-subscribe@lists.oreilly.com
Put the following information in the first line of your message (*not* in the Subject field):
subscribe ora-events

3. Get Examples from Our Books via FTP

There are two ways to access an archive of example files from our books:

Regular FTP
- ftp to:
  ftp.oreilly.com
  (login: anonymous
  password: your email address)
- Point your web browser to:
  ftp://ftp.oreilly.com/

FTPMAIL
- Send an email message to:
  ftpmail@online.oreilly.com
  (Write "help" in the message body)

4. Contact Us via Email

order@oreilly.com
To place a book or software order online. Good for North American and international customers.

subscriptions@oreilly.com
To place an order for any of our newsletters or periodicals.

books@oreilly.com
General questions about any of our books.

software@oreilly.com
For general questions and product information about our software. Check out O'Reilly Software Online at **http://software.oreilly.com/** for software and technical support information. Registered O'Reilly software users send your questions to:
website-support@oreilly.com

cs@oreilly.com
For answers to problems regarding your order or our products.

booktech@oreilly.com
For book content technical questions or corrections.

proposals@oreilly.com
To submit new book or software proposals to our editors and product managers.

international@oreilly.com
For information about our international distributors or translation queries. For a list of our distributors outside of North America check out:
http://www.oreilly.com/distributors.html

5. Work with Us

Check out our website for current employment opportunites:
http://jobs.oreilly.com/

O'Reilly & Associates, Inc.
101 Morris Street, Sebastopol, CA 95472 USA
TEL   707-829-0515 or 800-998-9938
       (6am to 5pm PST)
FAX   707-829-0104

International Distributors

http://international.oreilly.com/distributors.html

UK, EUROPE, MIDDLE EAST AND AFRICA (EXCEPT FRANCE, GERMANY, AUSTRIA, SWITZERLAND, LUXEMBOURG, AND LIECHTENSTEIN)

INQUIRIES
O'Reilly UK Limited
4 Castle Street
Farnham
Surrey, GU9 7HS
United Kingdom
Telephone: 44-1252-711776
Fax: 44-1252-734211
Email: information@oreilly.co.uk

ORDERS
Wiley Distribution Services Ltd.
1 Oldlands Way
Bognor Regis
West Sussex PO22 9SA
United Kingdom
Telephone: 44-1243-843294
UK Freephone: 0800-243207
Fax: 44-1243-843302 (Europe/EU orders)
or 44-1243-843274 (Middle East/Africa)
Email: cs-books@wiley.co.uk

GERMANY, SWITZERLAND, AUSTRIA, LUXEMBOURG, AND LIECHTENSTEIN

INQUIRIES & ORDERS
O'Reilly Verlag
Balthasarstr. 81
D-50670 Köln, Germany
Telephone: 49-221-973160-91
Fax: 49-221-973160-8
Email: anfragen@oreilly.de (inquiries)
Email: order@oreilly.de (orders)

FRANCE

INQUIRIES & ORDERS
Éditions O'Reilly
18 rue Séguier
75006 Paris, France
Tel: 33-1-40-51-52-30
Fax: 33-1-40-51-52-31
Email: france@oreilly.fr

CANADA (FRENCH LANGUAGE BOOKS)
Les Éditions Flammarion ltée
375, Avenue Laurier Ouest
Montréal (Québec) H2V 2K3
Tel: 00-1-514-277-8807
Fax: 00-1-514-278-2085
Email: info@flammarion.qc.ca

HONG KONG
City Discount Subscription Service, Ltd.
Unit A, 6th Floor, Yan's Tower
27 Wong Chuk Hang Road
Aberdeen, Hong Kong
Tel: 852-2580-3539
Fax: 852-2580-6463
Email: citydis@ppn.com.hk

KOREA
Hanbit Media, Inc.
Chungmu Bldg. 210
Yonnam-dong 568-33
Mapo-gu
Seoul, Korea
Tel: 822-325-0397
Fax: 822-325-9697
Email: hant93@chollian.dacom.co.kr

PHILIPPINES
Global Publishing
G/F Benavides Garden
1186 Benavides St.
Manila, Philippines
Tel: 632-254-8949/632-252-2582
Fax: 632-734-5060/632-252-2733
Email: globalp@pacific.net.ph

TAIWAN
O'Reilly Taiwan
1st Floor, No. 21, Lane 295
Section 1, Fu-Shing South Road
Taipei, 106 Taiwan
Tel: 886-2-27099669
Fax: 886-2-27038802
Email: mori@oreilly.com

CHINA
O'Reilly Beijing
SIGMA Building, Suite B809
No. 49 Zhichun Road
Haidian District
Beijing 100031, P.R. China
Tel: 86-10-8809-7475
Fax: 86-10-8809-7463
Email: beijing@oreilly.com

INDIA
Shroff Publishers & Distributors Pvt. Ltd.
12, "Roseland", 2nd Floor
180, Waterfield Road, Bandra (West)
Mumbai 400 050
Tel: 91-22-641-1800/643-9910
Fax: 91-22-643-2422
Email: spd@vsnl.com

JAPAN
O'Reilly Japan, Inc.
Yotsuya Y's Building
7 Banch 6, Honshio-cho
Shinjuku-ku
Tokyo 160-0003 Japan
Tel: 81-3-3356-5227
Fax: 81-3-3356-5261
Email: japan@oreilly.com

THAILAND
TransQuest Publishers (Thailand)
535/49 Kasemsuk Yaek 5
Soi Pracharat-Bampen 15
Huay Kwang, Bangkok
Thailand 10310
Tel: 662-6910421 or 6910638
Fax: 662-6902235
Email: puripat@.inet.co.th

ALL OTHER ASIAN COUNTRIES
O'Reilly & Associates, Inc.
101 Morris Street
Sebastopol, CA 95472 USA
Tel: 707-829-0515
Fax: 707-829-0104
Email: order@oreilly.com

AUSTRALIA
Woodslane Pty., Ltd.
7/5 Vuko Place
Warriewood NSW 2102
Australia
Tel: 61-2-9970-5111
Fax: 61-2-9970-5002
Email: info@woodslane.com.au

NEW ZEALAND
Woodslane New Zealand, Ltd.
21 Cooks Street (P.O. Box 575)
Waganui, New Zealand
Tel: 64-6-347-6543
Fax: 64-6-345-4840
Email: info@woodslane.com.au

ARGENTINA
Distribuidora Cuspide
Suipacha 764
1008 Buenos Aires
Argentina
Phone: 5411-4322-8868
Fax: 5411-4322-3456
Email: libros@cuspide.com

O'REILLY®

TO ORDER: **800-998-9938** • **order@oreilly.com** • **http://www.oreilly.com/**
OUR PRODUCTS ARE AVAILABLE AT A BOOKSTORE OR SOFTWARE STORE NEAR YOU.
FOR INFORMATION: **800-998-9938** • **707-829-0515** • **info@oreilly.com**

® O'REILLY

O'Reilly & Associates, Inc.
101 Morris Street
Sebastopol, CA 95472-9902
1-800-998-9938

Visit us online at:
www.oreilly.com
order@oreilly.com

O'REILLY WOULD LIKE TO HEAR FROM YOU

Which book did this card come from?

_____

Where did you buy this book?
- ❏ Bookstore
- ❏ Direct from O'Reilly
- ❏ Bundled with hardware/software
- ❏ Computer Store
- ❏ Class/seminar
- ❏ Other _____

What operating system do you use?
- ❏ UNIX
- ❏ Windows NT
- ❏ Macintosh
- ❏ PC(Windows/DOS)
- ❏ Other _____

What is your job description?
- ❏ System Administrator
- ❏ Network Administrator
- ❏ Web Developer
- ❏ Programmer
- ❏ Educator/Teacher
- ❏ Other _____

❏ Please send me O'Reilly's catalog, containing a complete listing of O'Reilly books and software.

Name _____   Company/Organization _____

Address _____

City _____   State _____   Zip/Postal Code _____   Country _____

Telephone _____   Internet or other email address (specify network) _____

Nineteenth century wood engraving
of a bear from the O'Reilly &
Associates Nutshell Handbook®
Using & Managing UUCP.

BUSINESS REPLY MAIL
FIRST CLASS MAIL   PERMIT NO. 80   SEBASTOPOL, CA

Postage will be paid by addressee

O'Reilly & Associates, Inc.
101 Morris Street
Sebastopol, CA 95472-9902